Cruise of the *Dashing Wave*

New Perspectives on Maritime History and Nautical Archaeology

UNIVERSITY PRESS OF FLORIDA

Florida A&M University, Tallahassee
Florida Atlantic University, Boca Raton
Florida Gulf Coast University, Ft. Myers
Florida International University, Miami
Florida State University, Tallahassee
New College of Florida, Sarasota
University of Central Florida, Orlando
University of Florida, Gainesville
University of North Florida, Jacksonville
University of South Florida, Tampa
University of West Florida, Pensacola

CRUISE OF THE DASHING WAVE

Rounding Cape Horn in 1860

Philip Hichborn

Edited by William H. Thiesen

Foreword by James C. Bradford and Gene Allen Smith

University Press of Florida

Gainesville/Tallahassee/Tampa/Boca Raton

Pensacola/Orlando/Miami/Jacksonville/Ft. Myers/Sarasota

15   14   13   12   11   10   6   5   4   3   2   1

Library of Congress Cataloging-in-Publication Data
Hichborn, Philip, 1839–1910.
Cruise of the Dashing Wave : rounding Cape Horn in
1860 / Philip Hichborn ; edited by William H. Thiesen;
foreword by James C. Bradford and Gene Allen Smith.
p. cm.
Includes bibliographical references and index.
ISBN 978-0-8130-3437-9 (alk. paper)
1. Hichborn, Philip, 1839-1910—Travel—Horn,
Cape (Chile) 2. Hichborn, Philip, 1839-1910—Diaries.
3. Sailors—Chile—Horn, Cape, Region—Biography.
4. Explorers—Chile—Horn, Cape, Region—History.
5. Voyages and travel—Horn, Cape (Chile) 6. Horn, Cape
(Chile)—Discovery and exploration. I. Thiesen, William H.
II. Title.
GV812.5.H53A3 2009
983'02—dc22   2009044791

The University Press of Florida is the scholarly publishing agency for the State University System of Florida,
comprising Florida A&M University, Florida Atlantic
University, Florida Gulf Coast University, Florida International University, Florida State University, New College of
Florida, University of Central Florida, University of Florida,
University of North Florida, University of South Florida,
and University of West Florida.

University Press of Florida
15 Northwest 15th Street
Gainesville, FL 32611-2079
http://www.upf.com

Dedicated to Philip Hichborn, who began his career as a ship's carpenter on *Dashing Wave* and rose through the ranks to become an admiral and the chief constructor of the U.S. Navy. His skill, determination, and leadership helped guide the navy's technological transformation from the Age of Sail to the Age of Steel, as the nation built a fleet of modern warships to replace its aging wooden sailing vessels. His devotion to friends, community, and family heritage motivated him to preserve for posterity the memories set down in this journal.

To all that may read this journal,
please make a reasonable allowance
for uncalled-for remarks, &c., &c., &c.

Yours respectfully, in haste,
PHILIP HICHBORN.

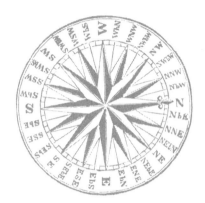

Contents

Foreword

~~~~~~

Water is unquestionably the most important natural feature on earth. By volume the world's oceans compose 99 percent of the planet's living space; in fact, the surface of the Pacific Ocean alone is larger than that of the total land bodies. Water is as vital to life as air. Indeed, to test whether the moon or other planets can sustain life, NASA looks for signs of water. The story of human development is inextricably linked to the oceans, seas, lakes, and rivers that dominate the earth's surface. The University Press of Florida's series *New Perspectives on Maritime History and Nautical Archaeology* is devoted to exploring the significance of the earth's water while providing lively and important books that cover the spectrum of maritime history and nautical archaeology broadly defined. The series includes works that focus on the role of canals, rivers, lakes, and oceans in history; on the economic, military, and political use of those waters; and upon the people, communities, and industries that support maritime endeavors. Limited by neither geography nor time, volumes in the series contribute to the overall understanding of maritime history and can be read with profit by both general readers and specialists.

At the beginning of the nineteenth century Americans knew little about California and the Pacific world. The land reportedly seemed salubrious and plentiful yet controlled by what many Americans considered an inefficient Spanish and then Mexican government and people. The South Pacific, which appeared as an exotic paradise of half-dressed island natives, would become increasingly important for American merchants and a fresh hunting ground for New England whalers by the 1820s. When Richard Henry Dana and Herman Melville vividly described the Pacific world during the 1840s, the area was in the midst of considerable change. European nations had dispatched explorers to the region during the late eighteenth century and were beginning to lay claim to various islands. Former Spanish colonies in Central and South America had gained independence but continued to be swept by disorder. To the north, California would be seized by the United States and begin to evolve from a sleepy Mexican province to an American territory, when the discovery of gold drew thousands to the region.

The forty-niners traveled to California via three routes: some trekked across the wide North American continent by land; others took ship from North Atlantic ports to Central America, crossed the steamy jungles of Panama to the Pacific, and boarded another ship for the voyage north to California; a third group traveled entirely by sea from the North Atlantic through the stormy passage around South America and north to San Francisco Bay. The trip was extremely dangerous, regardless of the route taken. Nor did it become significantly shorter or safer until the Panama Railroad was completed in 1855 and the transcontinental railroad spanned the United States in 1869. Until then, most freight and a significant number of individuals continued to travel to California by sea, and several left accounts of their journey.

Among the most graphic is Philip Hichborn's memoir of the 143-day 1860 cruise of the *Dashing Wave* "around the Horn." Hichborn, who had recently completed training as a theoretical ship designer and accepted a shipwright's position to work at the Mare Island naval base near San Francisco, signed aboard the clipper ship as a carpenter to cover the expenses of his trip from Boston to California. His account of the ensuing voyage goes well beyond that of other nineteenth-century maritime memoirs, logbooks, and diaries. While most travelers recorded only routine details of daily life—such as weather and sea conditions, cargo disposition, and occasional sea life sightings—Hichborn describes living conditions and social life aboard what was one of the nineteenth century's better-known clipper ships.

Hichborn's account is written not from the officer's nor the common seaman's perspective. His intermediate rank between the two allowed Hichborn to mingle among both groups. His work took him to all parts of the ship—he had constantly to inspect the clipper's wooden hull, fine tune her equipment, and adjust her riggings and sails—which broadened his opportunity to observe the officers, crewmen, and passengers. Hichborn records his experiences as a skilled technician on board the clipper ship, records the work of his fellow crewmen, and describes the reaction of passengers forced to endure the challenges of cold, wet, stormy weather.

William Thiesen discovered the journal "Cruise of the *Dashing Wave*" while researching his previous book on the history of American shipbuilding. Given the scarcity of memoirs by ships' carpenters combined with Hichborn's poignant observations about living and social conditions, this memoir sheds light on maritime life from a new perspective, that of a carpenter who performed his duties below deck, on deck, and up in the rigging despite the sea and weather conditions. Hichborn's skill and dedication to duty shine through the narrative. The conversational style of his memoir allows the reader to sail along with him and experience the mariner's life as Hichborn experienced it on board the *Dashing Wave*.

James C. Bradford and Gene Allen Smith
Series Editors

Introduction

~~~~~~

I discovered the journal "Cruise of the *Dashing Wave*" while researching at the National Archives for a book I was writing on the history of
American shipbuilding.[1] Written by ship's carpenter Philip Hichborn,
this unique personal journal enthralled me. Each page revealed the true
story of life and death on an 1860 clipper-ship voyage from Boston to
San Francisco by way of stormy Cape Horn. Many nineteenth-century
journals, logbooks, and diaries provide colorless lists of sailing data such
as date, time, and sea and weather conditions. In "Cruise of the *Dashing
Wave*," Hichborn focuses on the living conditions and social life aboard
one of the period's better-known clipper ships. His engaging conversational style allows the reader to sail along with him and experience the
mariner's life as he experienced it.[2]

Unlike most seafaring memoirs, this one is not written from the perspective of the captain, an officer, or a seaman sailing before the mast.
As *Dashing Wave*'s ship's carpenter, Philip Hichborn lacked the status
of an officer, yet he was considered a rank above the sailors who worked
the ship. Hichborn's diary provides an unusually personal perspective on
life aboard a nineteenth-century clipper ship, and his descriptions of his
duties as ship's carpenter add to the richness of his story.

During their day clipper ships were the thoroughbreds of the shipping
business, setting records for swift passages and racing other clippers for
the quickest times. More than any other crewmember, the ship's carpenter was responsible for the maintenance of these complex wind-driven
vessels. An endless task, this included repairs to the hull and below-decks
structures, deck houses, hatch covers, masts and spars, much of the running gear, ship's boats, and the myriad of other elements that comprised

---

1 *Industrializing American Shipbuilding* (University Press of Florida, 2006).
2 "Cruise of the *Dashing Wave*," Record Group 19, Records of the Bureau of Ships, Entry
   46, Box 1, National Archives and Records Administration, Washington, D.C.

Philip Hichborn pictured at the time of his 1860 passage on *Dashing Wave*. He is approximately twenty-one years old in this daguerreotype, copied from the original manuscript of "Cruise of the *Dashing Wave*." (Record Group 19: "Cruise of the *Dashing Wave*," National Archives and Records Administration, Washington, D.C.)

a large sailing ship. Hichborn performed this duty below decks, on deck, and high up in the rigging, even in the worst sea and weather conditions.

Ship's Carpenter Philip Hichborn

Before signing on to serve as *Dashing Wave*'s ship's carpenter, Philip Hichborn excelled in school and in professional training. Born in Boston, Massachusetts, on March 4, 1839, he was the second son of Martha Gould Hichborn and Philip Hichborn Sr., a relative of Paul Revere and a shipwright in the Boston Navy Yard.[3] The younger Hichborn was one of only two boys to graduate from Charlestown High School in 1855.

---

3   Hichborn, "Chronology," 2–5.

After high school Hichborn began working at the Boston Navy Yard and entered night school at the local French's Mercantile Agency. He began serving as assistant secretary to the Navy Yard's commandant, Captain Francis H. Gregory, and within a year he was indentured to master shipwright Melvin Simmons as a shipwright's apprentice. Hichborn successfully completed his apprenticeship and impressed Commandant Gregory with his skills and knowledge. Gregory recommended Hichborn for further education and, on orders from Treasury Secretary Isaac Toucey, he received special training in theoretical ship design and construction.[4]

The year 1860 proved an important one for Hichborn. He celebrated his twenty-first birthday, completed training at the Navy Yard, and graduated from French's with a commemorative gold-colored broad axe in recognition of his excellent academic record. In July of that year, the navy appointed Melvin Simmons as naval constructor and ordered him to Mare Island Naval Shipyard near San Francisco. Simmons offered Hichborn a shipwright's position at Mare Island, which his former apprentice accepted. To make his passage from Boston to San Francisco, Hichborn signed on as ship's carpenter aboard the clipper ship *Dashing Wave*.[5]

Clipper Ship *Dashing Wave*

Dashing Wave proved to be one of the most durable clipper ships ever built. On July 14, 1853, Portsmouth, New Hampshire's Fernald & Pettigrew Shipyard completed *Dashing Wave*, which received an "A1" clipper ship rating with an original registered tonnage of approximately 1,200 tons. She measured a little over 180 feet in length, with a thirty-eight-foot beam and a nineteen-foot draft. With a working lifespan of over sixty-six years, *Dashing Wave* would outlive nearly all other wooden clipper ships.[6]

After *Dashing Wave*'s completion, the Boston merchant house of Samuel Tilton & Company took possession of the ship and assigned Captain John Fiske to command her. In the fall of 1853 Fiske captained the clip-

4   See Skerrett, "Philip Hichborn," *Cassier's*, 140, and Hamersly, 389–90.
5   Skerrett, "Philip Hichborn," *Cassier's*, 141, and Hamersly, 390.
6   See Brighton, 88, and Fairburn, vol. 3, 1889.

Pen and ink sketch of *Dashing Wave* found in the original manuscript of "Cruise of the *Dashing Wave*." (Record Group 19: "Cruise of the *Dashing Wave*," National Archives and Records Administration, Washington, D.C.)

per on her first voyage, from Boston to San Francisco by way of Cape Horn. From there Fiske sailed the ship around the globe, returning to Boston by way of Calcutta. During her career as a high-seas sailing vessel, *Dashing Wave* periodically voyaged to the Pacific and Indian oceans, with port calls in Australia and India. In 1857, for example, *Dashing Wave* sustained heavy damage near India that required a port call to Calcutta for extensive repairs.[7]

Also known as the *Wave*, *Dashing Wave* did not make the swiftest passages. She made six trips to San Francisco by way of Cape Horn, most of them beginning in Boston. Her best passage, 107 days, took place in 1858, but the average duration for the six voyages was a little over 120 days. *Dashing Wave*'s 1860 voyage, recounted in this memoir, began on August 15 and ended January 5, 1861. The passage took 143 days and represented the vessel's longest nonstop passage from Boston to San Francisco. *Dashing Wave* was not the only vessel to experience poor sailing conditions that year. Of the six other clipper ships that rounded Cape Horn at the

---

7   Brighton, 91.

same time as *Dashing Wave*, nearly all took between 139 and 143 days to arrive at San Francisco.[8]

Unlike steamships, sailing ship passages were affected by the skills and personalities of their masters. *Dashing Wave*'s best passage to San Francisco was made the year before Hichborn's cruise. As Hichborn makes clear in his narrative, the ship's captain drove his crew and his carpenter, but he did not drive his ship. He displayed a caution unusual in an experienced master, and his reluctance to carry a full press of sail in any but the finest weather was quite frustrating to Hichborn and the crew, who were dismayed by the ever-lengthening duration of the voyage.

The difficulties *Dashing Wave* experienced in rounding the Horn, the working of her seams, the need for continual pumping, the rotten timbers requiring repair and recaulking, and the lack of necessary tools, supplies, and repair materials, certainly suggest that on this voyage, at least, *Dashing Wave* was not well provisioned and that the owners had failed to maintain her in good repair. At one point Hichborn observed that "there is no place around the bow that is not entirely rotten."

Captain David R. Lecraw

Hichborn's principal antagonist aboard *Dashing Wave*, the curmudgeonly captain, David R. Lecraw, took command of the clipper ship in 1859. Lecraw was born in 1804 to a seafaring family in Marblehead, Massachusetts. His brothers commanded ships of their own, and he had charge of other vessels before taking command of *Dashing Wave*. In 1835 Lecraw married Hannah Russell Girdler, and they had three children. Hannah accompanied Lecraw on some of his voyages, but she did not join him on Hichborn's cruise. During Hichborn's passage Lecraw brought along his pet dog, which died off the coast of Brazil before the ship reached Cape Horn.[9]

Most of the crew aboard *Dashing Wave* disliked Captain Lecraw. In his mid-fifties when he began serving as captain (one year before Hichborn's cruise), he was considered old by the seafaring standards of the day. According to Hichborn, Lecraw was feared by the mates and disliked

8   Brighton, 88; Fairburn, vol. 5, 3086.
9   Lindsey, 84; Fairburn, vol. 6, 3941.

Clipper ship *Dashing Wave* in San Francisco Bay. Photograph circa 1900. (Photograph courtesy of the J. Porter Shaw Library, San Francisco Maritime National Historical Park.)

Daguerreotype image of Captain David R. Lecraw, likely taken before the 1860 passage around Cape Horn. (Courtesy of Marblehead Museum and Historical Society, Marblehead, Massachusetts.)

by almost everyone else aboard *Dashing Wave*. Even a passenger on the cruise before Hichborn's referred to Lecraw as an "old fogy."[10]

Lecraw was not a physically brutal man, as were the bully masters and "bucko" mates so prevalent in the nineteenth-century merchant fleet, but he was relentlessly demanding. Hichborn despised Lecraw, who seemed to take pleasure in devising every sort of carpentry project to fill the carpenter's waking hours. He granted Hichborn little rest and even less appreciation for the quality of his work. Lecraw must have trusted Hichborn, however, for he allowed the carpenter to clean and repair his pistols, a task that temporarily left him defenseless against the disaffected crew.

Hichborn also makes clear that the captain's obsessive parsimony contributed to the poor condition of the vessel and also to the hardships experienced by carpenter and crew. As Alan Villiers observes in *The Way*

---

10   See appendix C, "Remarks, about Ship *Dashing Wave*."

of a Ship, a good captain is sensitive to the well-being of his crew, both in terms of their victuals and also with regard to their living conditions.[11] In these matters Captain Lecraw seems to have been delinquent. A difficult master with an unhappy ship.

Crew of the *Dashing Wave*

The crew of a clipper ship had its own distinctive social order, and a mariner's rank and status dictated whether he lived in the forecastle, a deckhouse, or the officers' quarters. The 1860 crew of *Dashing Wave* comprised over thirty men and boys. Seamen lived in the forecastle, and the remainder of the crew occupied the forward house, a deckhouse located between the forecastle and the after cabin.

The officers included the captain and the first, second, and third mates. Hichborn never mentions their names, except that of the second mate, whom the captain called "Mr. Maynard." The officers were housed in the after cabin (or "after house") where, along with the captain, they took their meals.

Located between the officers' quarters and the forecastle, the forward house contained the galley, a cabin for ship's cook Moses Pearson, and a cabin for Hichborn, the sailmaker, and three "boys" (John Warriner, Charles "Charley" Howard, and another boy referred to only as "James" or "Jim"). On a nineteenth-century sailing vessel the title "boy" indicated a mariner with little experience; however, most boys tended to be teenagers or young men. On the second day out of Boston, the crew discovered two young stowaways, Frank Preston and Andrew J. Cate, so *Dashing Wave* carried five boys on the voyage. The three hired boys and the sailmaker occupied the same cabin as Hichborn, a space ordinarily occupied by four persons, while the two stowaways found bunk space in the forecastle with the ordinary seamen.

In addition to Captain Lecraw and the mates, Hichborn focuses most of his commentary regarding the crew on the hired boys and the sailmaker, probably because they shared his cabin space during the long passage and he came to know them better than other members of the crew.

---

11   See especially, 190–91.

While Hichborn mentioned the name of the cook, Moses Pearson, he never revealed the name of the sailmaker, referring to him only as "the sailmaker."

The rest of the crew consisted of two dozen seamen who occupied the forecastle and worked watches aboard the ship. The seamen were divided into two watches. The captain and the second mate oversaw the second mate's watch, also known as the "starboard" or "captain's watch," and the first and third mates oversaw the mate's watch, also known as the "port watch."

During the mid-nineteenth century, American clipper ships often employed many European seamen. American crewmembers on *Dashing Wave* referred to all of the foreigners as "Dutchmen," even though these men came from a variety of countries. Most of the Americans hailed from New England. For example, two of the seamen came from Rhode Island. The officers came mainly from Massachusetts: Captain Lecraw lived in Marblehead; the first mate hailed from Salem; and the third mate probably came from Boston. In addition to Hichborn, the two stowaways grew up in the Boston area, while the hired boy John Warriner hailed from Springfield, Massachusetts.

Hichborn had good relations with *Dashing Wave's* crew, with the exception of the captain, the first mate, the cook, and the sailmaker. He formed particularly close relationships with the second and third mates, the boys, and several of the American seamen. He probably did not have much interaction with the foreign sailors, making little mention of them in his journal. During the second half of the cruise, Hichborn took an active role in working the sails and going aloft, even though his position as ship's carpenter did not require him to do so. Working side by side with the rest of the seamen, he earned the respect of his shipmates and became a popular crewmember.

Life Aboard *Dashing Wave*

Life aboard *Dashing Wave* was physically demanding and dangerous, especially for the seamen who served before the mast. With the possible exception of the cook, every task carried out by seamen on *Dashing Wave* required physical strength and, especially aloft, a high degree of agility and coordination. Pumping the bilges, for example, was an arduous, tedious job the crew had to perform every day. When heavy seas came on board or hull seams worked open and allowed in ocean water, manning the pumps could become an exhausting nightmare.

As was typical of all nineteenth-century sailing ships, there were no safety regulations to protect seamen from the dangers of their tasks and from abuse by the captain and the mates. Life could be especially harsh in naval vessels, and the nineteenth-century merchant navy was little better. Legislation to protect seamen on American ships was only grudgingly enacted long after the need for it became apparent.

When men went aloft, they wore no safety harnesses as do modern tall-ship sailors. Furling sails was a highly hazardous operation: sailors moved out along the yards, standing only on a single footrope—often without a safety line behind them to catch them if a billowing sail threatened to blow them off the yard. Survival, especially in heavy weather, required strength, courage, and quick reflexes. The safeguard advised by common wisdom, "one hand for the ship and one for yourself," was often impossible, and many a man either fell to his death on the deck or was blown over the side as the wind caught a partially furled sail. Few of the men owned gloves, so their hands blistered, peeled, cracked open, and bled from hard use and continual exposure to salt water, rough canvas, and the elements.

In rounding Cape Horn, *Dashing Wave's* seamen were pushed to their physical limits by foul weather and heavy seas, their watches often punctuated by moments of fear and despair. During the 1860 passage, *Dashing Wave* spent well over a month battling rough seas, headwinds, rain, snow, sleet, and bone-chilling cold, just trying to "make her westing" and safely round the Horn. At one point during this struggle, the clipper almost wrecked, and one stormy night it nearly collided with another sailing vessel.

The contrary winds and heavy seas required almost nonstop work aloft and on deck. Continuous work in numbingly cold conditions sapped the strength of the entire crew, and fatigue caused numerous injuries and one death. A passage round the Horn is hard on any vessel, and sailing ships

Seamen working aloft on the yards of a square-rigged ship. Note the lack of gloves worn by the seamen. (Photograph courtesy of the United States Coast Guard.)

were especially vulnerable to damage to their spars and rigging. As ship's carpenter, Hichborn's work in maintaining and repairing *Dashing Wave* was critically important, and here his skill and tenacity served him, and his ship, well.

Crews wore oilskin clothing to protect themselves from heavy weather, but oilskins were ineffective when heavy seas came on board, and they provided little warmth compared to modern water-resistant sailing gear. In foul weather, seamen were wet and cold all the time and had no means to dry their clothing and other gear. The constant exposure to salt water covered Hichborn's shipmates with welts, boils, and ugly sores.

The food aboard ship served as the main distraction from the routine of shipboard life and was a constant preoccupation for the crew. Hichborn found the ship's diet important enough to include a copy of the weekly menu at the end of his journal. According to Hichborn's "Bill of

Fare" (see appendix B), the cook served the same food each day of the week, with little change in the weekly regimen. The crew received a diet rich in carbohydrates, especially potatoes. For protein, *Dashing Wave's* cook Moses Pearson relied on salt beef and fresh pork provided by the live pigs penned on deck. Occasionally the men would catch a porpoise to supplement their diet. Hichborn gained a considerable amount of weight due to this diet, outgrowing his clothes, and his face fattened so much that his shipmates thought he suffered from tooth problems and a swollen jaw. Despite the calorie-rich food, the diet lacked necessary vitamins and fresh fruit, and toward the end of the passage, Hichborn began to notice signs of scurvy among his shipmates.

Except for the military, few nineteenth-century working environments threw together so diverse a group of strangers and expected them to work and live together under such difficult conditions, twenty-four hours a day, seven days a week, for voyages of uncertain duration with little if any opportunity for respite or escape. The confined living conditions and lack of privacy on clipper ships like *Dashing Wave* led to tense relationships among crewmembers. Fights broke out between the Americans and the so-called Dutchmen. No democracy existed on these vessels, only orders to be obeyed without question. And while the men disliked Captain Lecraw, they loathed the first mate, occasionally threatening him with violence should he push them too far. In the end, the crew had to pull together as a team despite their differences. This proved especially true while rounding Cape Horn, where *Dashing Wave's* crew struggled for survival against the storms and gales typical of those waters. Commenting on *Dashing Wave's* cruise, Hichborn's biographer, Robert Skerrett, wrote: "He witnessed the stages from neglected sickness and accidental death to something just this side of mutiny and murder, and learned the lessons of considerate management and self-control."[12]

Despite the length and difficulties of the voyage, Hichborn appears to have done well, even (to his dismay) gaining a good deal of weight. His skill, self-discipline, integrity, and perseverance were to stand him in good stead throughout his naval career. Although inexperienced, Hichborn clearly was a fine, intuitive seaman.

---

12   "Philip Hichborn," *Cassier's*, 141.

◆

Transcribing the faded type on the pages of "Cruise of the *Dashing Wave*" has been a difficult task, but it also has been a rewarding one. Hichborn's words and phrasing often are colloquial but, as such, convey the expressions used by ordinary seamen who sailed the high seas during the midnineteenth century. I have therefore preserved the diction and stylings of Philip Hichborn's journal (and of related original documents reproduced in the appendixes), occasionally altering syntax and punctuation for the sake of consistency and readability. I also have retained certain parenthetical items left behind by the transcriber who typed the handwritten journal, placing them in brackets.[13] In sum, then, the substance of the diary remains quite intact, much as Hichborn wrote it almost 150 years ago.

Hichborn's original handwritten journal never has surfaced, therefore it is impossible to compare the typescript with his original manuscript. Although we assume some reasonable diligence and accuracy on the part of the typist, we do not know if the copy in the National Archives is accurate in every detail or if it was read and approved by Hichborn. In short, provenance cannot be established with certainty. We also do not know if Hichborn intended to publish the typed version that is presented here or if he simply wanted to preserve his diary in a more legible form for his family or future generations.

I have augmented Hichborn's narrative with a track chart indicating the route taken by *Dashing Wave* on her voyage from Boston to San Francisco. It is based on coordinates and land sightings noted in the text. The initial leg of the voyage took the ship to the eastern Atlantic before she turned south. This apparently lengthy detour was not uncommon for sailing ships wanting to avoid the Gulf Stream, which flowed north along most of the Atlantic seaboard.

With the exception of Hichborn's first reported latitude and longitude, most of the early notations only give the latitude. *Dashing Wave* had

---

13   The identity of the transcriptionist and the date of the typescript are unknown. As to the latter, a general time frame can be deduced: the manuscript was typed sometime between the invention of the typewriter around 1867 (the first commercially successful model went on the market in 1873) and Philip Hichborn's retirement from the navy in 1901.

a good navigational quadrant, and even the boys had learned to take the latitude; but only the mate possessed a marine chronometer of sufficient accuracy to determine longitude with precision. Hichborn wrote of him, "I could easily get the longitude were I to ask the mate, but I do not like him well enough to speak to him unless it is absolutely necessary."

In any case, longitude was not of great concern in the early stages of the voyage and only became critical when *Dashing Wave* made first landfall at Pernambuco and, of course, when it rounded the Horn. Then it was necessary to know, or to estimate, longitude with some accuracy before a prudent captain would make that all-important turn to starboard and head his vessel north. By the time the ship reached the Pacific Ocean, Hichborn noted both latitude and longitude. Keeping in mind that San Francisco lies approximately fifty-five degrees west of Cape Horn, it seems reasonable that Hichborn's diary now reflected as much interest in *Dashing Wave*'s westerly progress as in how far north she was.

Dashing Wave finally arrived in San Francisco on January 5, 1861, after a voyage of 143 days.[14] Hichborn's diary is silent on his activities after disembarking, and many details of his personal life after *Dashing Wave* (for example, his residence, his friends, and so on) are unknown to us. We pick up his life's story as he begins his tenure at Mare Island Shipyard (see appendix D).

In addition to the photographs and illustrations woven into the text, I have added several useful appendixes. These include a glossary of nautical and slang terms, a *Dashing Wave* sail chart, and accounts by *Dashing Wave* passengers of their experiences aboard the clipper ship. The bibliography provides references to other nineteenth-century seafaring memoirs, including a few accounts that describe sailing passages around Cape Horn. The bibliography also includes a brief list of scholarly works focusing on the social history of nineteenth-century sailing vessels, and other sources of information for Philip Hichborn and *Dashing Wave*.

In "Cruise of the *Dashing Wave*," Philip Hichborn has written more than just a colorful history of an ocean voyage. His journal serves as a time capsule, taking the reader back to the days when the clipper ship

---

14   See Fairburn, vol. 5, 3086.

truly was the Queen of the Seas. Back to a world that traces its traditions, customs, and culture to the wooden vessels of antiquity. Philip Hichborn gives voice to those hardy souls who went down to the sea in ships and provides twenty-first-century readers with a highly personal insight into the hardships, the challenges, and the rewards of rounding the Horn in a nineteenth-century clipper ship.

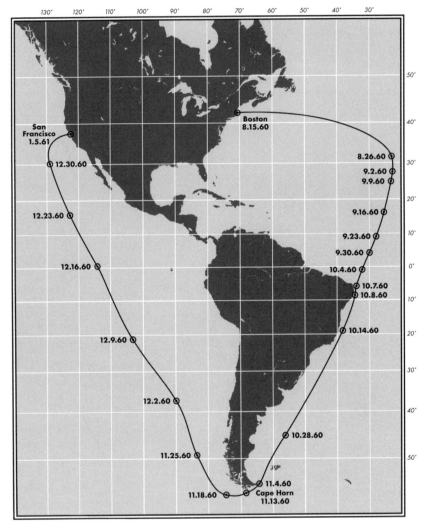

Track chart indicating the route taken by *Dashing Wave* on her voyage from Boston to San Francisco based on coordinates and land sightings noted in the text. By taking an extreme eastward track after leaving Boston, *Dashing Wave* avoided the northerly current of the Gulf Stream. The Gulf Stream flows eastward from about the latitude of Nantucket, and *Dashing Wave* would have taken advantage of that. (Drawing by Mary H. Thiesen.)

CRUISE OF THE
DASHING WAVE

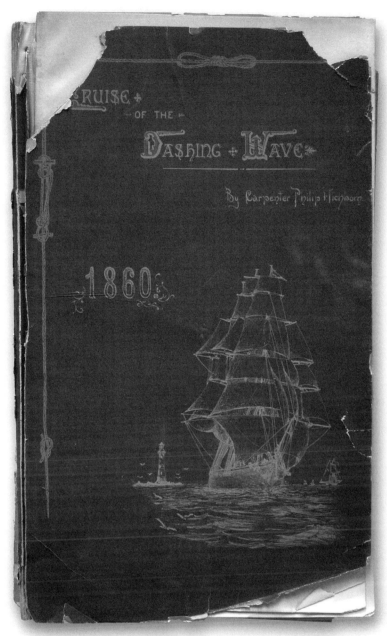

Original hand-drawn cover of the manuscript "Cruise of the *Dashing Wave*," showing the clipper ship passing Minot's Ledge Lighthouse south of Boston. (Record Group 19: "Cruise of the *Dashing Wave*," National Archives and Records Administration, Washington, D.C.)

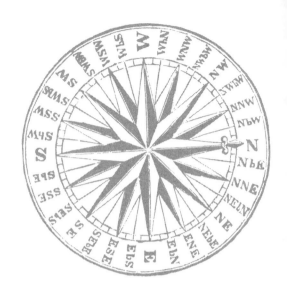

August 15, 1860.

As Carpenter of the Ship.

Started from Boston with a North-west wind; parted company with the tow-boat at 1:30 o'clock, and bid farewell to friends.

The first work for the carpenter was to assist in getting the ship under way, pulling and hauling at anything that became necessary.

Toward afternoon, the ship was about off Minot's Ledge, and then I went to work putting parcelling and battens around the edge of the booby-hatch, which took some time on account of every thing being new. The captain came to me where I was working and said, "Well, carpenter ain't you got that hatch done yet." He remarked that he could do it himself in fifteen minutes.

About this time I began to feel a little discouraged in my stomach, and night time coming on, I turned in to sleep for the first time aboard the ship. Being tired and sleepy, I knew nothing until the morning.

Upon turning out, the ship was rolling so that it was almost impossible for me to stand on deck, so I turned into my berth again and slept all that day and the night following.

August 17th, 1860.

The Captain sent for me. I turned out, and upon going to him he told me to make a staff for the dog-vane; but I told him that I was not able to work, to which he replied by giving me permission to lay off for the day.

August 18th, 1860.

The wind is blowing quite fresh, a reef has been taken in the mizzen top-sail. I did a little carpentering about the ship this day, driving the pins out of the shackles of the chain, and other small jobs. Being sick all the time it was almost impossible for me to move at all, accordingly I improved every opportunity to sit down; my favorite position being on the step of the door where I lived. One thing I omitted was, on the morning of the 17th it was discovered that two boys had stowed themselves away aboard the ship before we started.

The captain called them aft at eight bells, and asked them how they came to stow themselves away aboard the ship, and told them first that he would hang them up in the rigging, but afterwards told them that they should work the whole passage; then they were sent forward.

The stowaways proved to be Charles Emerson of Boston, aged 19, and Andrew J. Cate of Charlestown. The former's name subsequently proved to be Frank Preston. Cate was 16 years of age. He told me next day that he lived in Charlestown on Allston Street, and that he knew all of my brothers. I asked him on Sunday evening how he liked going to sea, to which he replied, "Oh my, I wish that I were at home."

The boys had only such clothing as they stood in, and while stowed away they were sick several times, so that you can imagine how nice and clean they looked.

Charles Emerson, or rather Frank Preston, was put in the mate's watch with me, while Andrew Cate was in the second-mate's watch.

The sailors gave them a few clothes and allowed them to sleep in their berths.

August 19th, 1860.

Being Sunday, I turned out and washed myself, feeling better than any day before. Nothing of any account transpired during the day. All the men and boys were lying about talking of home. I don't think there was hardly another person aboard but who felt worse than I did; for having been sick, I felt refreshed on recovering.

August 20th, 1860.

I opened the fore hatch, which being a very bad one, proved quite a job for me. It took six bails of oakum to caulk it. To pay it, I had to heat the pitch, and to do that I was obliged to use the galley, a thing which made

Dashing Wave *off Boston Light, 1855*, painting by William Bradford. (Courtesy of the Peabody Essex Museum, Salem, Massachusetts.)

the cook swear like a pirate. I thought to myself, "old nigger if I had you ashore and you talked that way to me, I would twist your nose off." He is the worst old growl that ever came aboard a ship.

I was so sick this day that I could hardly stand; nevertheless, I kept at work but began to think that I should never get over my sea-sickness, although there were others aboard, even to the sailors, who were quite as sick. Up to this time I had eaten nothing, and had no appetite at all. The mate told the cook to make me a little gruel which, having eaten, I began to gain strength and appetite very fast. Once the captain came into my room and asked me how I was getting along.

August 21st, 1860.

I finished the dog-vane staff for the captain, and commenced the work of making wooden handles for the buckets.

22nd, August, 1860.

The carpenter is now all right, and the work has now commenced in earnest, enough to keep me busy all the time, five or six jobs at once.

August 23rd, 1860.

The first time aloft, to nail on a staff under the main-top, the ship rolling and tumbling, and under reefed topsails fore and aft.

August 24th, 1860.

Aloft again to nail on a piece on the cross-trees; a little easier than at first and a beautiful sight as far as one could see.

During the first week we passed two ships and a brig, the latter coming so near that we could see the men on deck.

August 25th, 1860.

Being Saturday, I worked until four o'clock in the afternoon making battens, and then commenced to clean my tools.

As a general thing I turn out at six o'clock in the morning and work until 7:30 o'clock, then get breakfast, which I eat off of the top of my tool chest, after which I commence work a little past eight o'clock, continuing until twelve. We are allowed one hour at dinner, after which I return to my duties and work until tea time; after tea lay off and have a smoke, turning in about nine P.M.

Sunday, Aug. 26th, 1860.

This is the day that I commenced to write this journal, it being the first chance that I have had. I turned out this morning, washed, shaved, and dressed myself up a little, which made me feel like a new man. I have on a blue checked shirt, black pants, and patent-leather shoes.

The weather is quite warm, being in latitude 32N, longitude 23W, but a person cannot realize themselves being so far away from home, as the sea looks the same to them all the time. I occasionally have to think of what is going on in Charlestown; but no more than possible, it is not at all agreeable just now. I think I never have had a better appetite in my life than now, it seems as though I could not eat enough, and I am anxious for meal time to come around. Upon the whole thus far I am as contented as I expected, but have made up my mind to leave the ship in San Francisco; she proving to be a very weak and leaky vessel, having to pump ship every four hours. In a head sea she makes 18 inches in that interval. They sound the pumps every watch.

My station in the tacking ship is to attend to the spanker. If the ship holds together to get around the Cape, this voyage, in my opinion, will be her last, unless they strengthen her considerably. The mate was overheard to say if we got her into 'Frisco we will be lucky.

I have no bed clothes on me of nights, it being warm enough without them. The officers and men treat me with respect, but the captain is a very dignified [reserved] sort of man, thus far hardly speaking a word to anyone. I washed a few clothes and mended my pants, after which I sat down forward to watch the motion of the ship. My books and papers are in great demand. I have lent quite a number to the third mate, who says he cannot possibly shake off the homesickness.

There is one man sick in the forecastle. Charles Howard was taken with the colic a few days out, but is now quite well. John Warriner, of Springfield, Mass, is the other boy who shipped on the wharf, without even going home to prepare himself in any way, coming aboard just as he stood. This addition makes five in the room, the agreement being only four.

They are a pretty good set of boys and behave themselves quite decently; keeping the room clean and listening earnestly to me when I advise them in regard to going to sea, i.e., to let the sea alone and stay ashore.

I got out a good many of my things today, and showed them to the boys, which amused them very much; in doing this I first discovered a piece of perforated paper and ribbon on which was worked the name of

"Sister," which took me all aback. I had thought of her, however, when I ate that cake she gave me to take with me. When I bite a piece off it tastes so good it makes my jaws go "hip up to do."

The 24th was the first time that I had a smoke, and then I smoked one of those cigars which Ned gave me, and enjoyed it more than any cigar that I had ever smoked before in my life. As it is now nearly supper time, I will have to cut short here by saying that it is a very beautiful day, but a head wind.

August 27th, 1860.

A dog-house to make. Lowered over the bow on a plank to look for a leak in the wood ends; found them soft on the port bow.

August 28th, 1860.

Setting in nails around the forward house.

August 29th, 1860.

Setting in nails around after house. It has been said often today, "Well carpenter, we are a fortnight out."

August 30th, 1860.

Setting in nails and putting in new plugs where there are signs of rot.

August 31st, 1860.

Setting in nails, repairing blocks, and other small jobs.

Sept. 1, 1860.

Drew the box in the starboard pumps, packed it anew, and thus far it goes well.

Sept. 2, 1860.

As this is the third Sunday that I have been aboard a ship, it is to be supposed that I am getting well accustomed to it. I got up this morning at 5:30 o'clock, washed myself all over and some of my clothes also. After breakfast, I shaved, put on a clean undershirt, and dressed myself in a brown checked shirt, white duck pants, etc. I then felt quite refreshed. There is a little of every thing going on today. For the last week the weather has been splendid, but the wind light and dead ahead all the time. Thus far we have only reached the latitude of 27°27′N, which is the only objection that offers itself.

It is a most splendid day, and several times I have queried in my mind, what was going on at home, but as to myself, to look at me, you would think I was perfectly at home, and take things quite cool, for the reason that I have some object in view besides going to sea for a living. If everything should continue as lovely for the future as it has for the past, I shall never regret the day I came to sea. The work that I have to do is of all descriptions: coopering, carpentering, blacksmithing, etc. One remark that is often made by the crew is "Do you mind how fat the carpenter is getting?" I guess that is so, for I cannot button my pants around me by 2 inches.

One thing is certain, however, no matter how well Charlestown people are enjoying themselves they cannot present a more splendid appearance than does the ship as she goes plunging through the sea, the spray flying on each bow. You may judge of my feelings when I say that knowing as much as I do now, and were I on Lewis' wharf I should be just as anxious to go. After a person has been this length of time aboard it seems to him a second nature; he becomes perfectly contented through its seeming naturalness and constancy, as a matter of course.

The second mate told me that any books in the cabin were at my pleasure, but thus far I have as many books as I can possibly read, and have not occasion to borrow.

As yet, they have given me no job but that I could do easily, and what I have done, has always given satisfaction; and the mate often says, "Well, that is first rate."

Today, I got the sailmaker quite mad, and as I have commented about him will give you my opinion of the man. He is one of those half breeders that you often see at home. He is considered by all to be the smartest man aboard [except 30], he is a regular blower, and the laziest man that I have ever seen. I see there is not a man aboard who likes him. Besides being lazy; he is also nasty, seldom if ever washing himself or his dishes. The first night out he got acquainted with all hands forward, [he thought he was something] telling all around what he was going to do and what he was not, and particularly that he was not going to mend sails aloft, &c. In a day or so the mate ordered him aloft to mend the main royal. If you had but seen the countenance he displayed, you would have laughed. After two or three attempts to get up, he finally reached the yard, the mate and all hands on deck laughing at him. When he came down the mate asked him why he hadn't buttoned himself to the yard. He had not been out a week, before one of the sailors was going to thrash him, which frightened him almost to death. He has more slang expressions than any person that I ever heard talk before; he also thinks that he is very handsome, and keeps a glass in his hand every chance he can get. He got mad with me for dividing the victuals; he used to sit down, and if there was anything nice, make a meal of it, and leave none for the rest. But I soon taught him that he had no greeny to deal with, which makes him as humble as a cat now. I have known him to lie in his berth all day long, saying he was sick, but when none of the officers were about he was well enough. As soon as anything ails him, he thinks he is going to die.

Sunday, Sept. 9th, 1860.

The day is very pleasant, and as this is the fourth Sunday aboard, I am becoming more and more reconciled. We still continue to have a head wind, and very light at that. Today we are in latitude 25°44'N, having only gone about 80 miles on our course during the past week; but I am in hopes it will be made up by fair winds before long. I have a job to set some pieces around the lower mast-head to steady the truss for the lower topsail yard, which will take two or three days; if I had to do it ashore, I should consider it impossible. Take the stock in your hands, tie your tools around your neck, and hold on to the rigging with your legs, etc.

I suppose you would like to know at home what I am doing to-day, and whether I am well or not, but I assure you I was never better in my life than I am at present. I cannot say that I am at all satisfied with the manner of living, but I do not mind it much when I consider it is only for the passage. I dreamed of home the other night for the first time since I came away; I should really like to know the thoughts of those at home.

On Saturday, we passed a brig, and I assure you she was quite a curiosity, not having seen a vessel since the one I mentioned last.

I overhauled my chest today, and gave my clothes a good airing, and looked at the daguerreotype, which I do not do very often because it makes me a little homesick.

I suppose by this time there is beginning to be some stir in politics round Boston; but I do not, as yet, enter into conversations of much account with anyone on board. Charlie Howard is the favorite with me, and thus far I find him to be a nice boy.

As Wednesday comes around you always hear remarked, "Two or three weeks, boys [as the case may be] since we started." The captain says that if we do not get some rain on the Line we will have to be on an allowance of water.

I took a good salt-water bath this morning before breakfast, or about five o'clock, which no doubt would seem early at home. Thus far I have had plenty of sleep, only having been called out once in the night since I started.

I am sitting on a spare yard beside a water cask, writing this. I have become so fat in the face that three or four have asked me if I had the tooth-ache, for my face appears as though it must be swollen.

The men all say that this is the most curious ship that they were ever in, you can hardly hear a sound on deck on Sunday.

Two bells are sounding for supper.

Sunday, September 16th, 1860.

The weather is very pleasant and agreeable, but at home it would seem melting.

I turned out this morning and took my usual sea bath, which stands awaiting me on the forecastle deck, in the form of the third mate with buckets of water which he throws upon me.

This morning the main-skysail burst. It was sent down, but the captain did not allow any work to be done on it today; a state of affairs perfectly agreeable to the sailmaker, who by the way is the laziest, and most contemptible pimp aboard the ship, and thoroughly despised by the officers and crew. As I have said before, he thinks himself very handsome, and the other day he went to Andrew, the little stowaway boy, and asked him if he did not think that he [the sailmaker] was handsome. Being too lazy to wash his dishes, he scrapes them around with his hand, and lets them go at that. It is lucky for him that he is in the second mate's watch, who, by the way, being a religious and quiet man, is so disgusted with him that he hardly speaks. But it takes the mate to make him step around; every chance he gets he sends him aloft.

The other night we had a squall. The sailmaker is no officer although he stands a regular watch. I had just finished work and was eating supper alone; at this time the sailmaker was in the room when he ought to have been on deck. Several orders were given at once, and the crew were running above, fore and aft. During this time the sailmaker was taking as long as possible to get into his oil-clothes, and when he had them on he stepped one foot out the door he promptly drew it back again, and said, "Oh dear it is going to blow" and then fairly hid himself away frightened, fearing to go on deck. He can see more black clouds and gales than any other man aboard the ship. Sometimes I am mad enough to knock him down, for I cannot go a man who is as brave as a lion when it is calm, and as much frightened and cowardly when it blows as he is brave in fair weather. When it blows a little he is ready to drop on his knees and pray. The weakness of his knees is not the result of piety but rather the effect of shameful cowardice. He brags of owing board money in Boston. I think when we reach 'Frisco, they will discharge him. At any rate, if I were to continue on ship he would have to go, I wouldn't sail with him again. The men are all of them anxious to have me thrash him, but he has not spunk enough to resent anything or I would have had him polished off before this time.

The boy Cate, as I have mentioned before, lived in Allston Street. He is a very queer sort of boy, particularly in the expressions he uses; an "old head." He often comes into my room and I talk with him. He says that what money he and his brother earn they are going to give to their mother to alter the house with; this he says with all possible seriousness. He, like the rest of the boys, is aboard the ship working without the prospect of pay. He remarked that when he got to 'Frisco, if the captain didn't give him some money he would take it out of the captain's hide; he is afraid of no one, cares for nothing, and is in the second mate's watch. The other stowaway is a very smart boy. He says his mother is an actress and used to play at the Boston Museum. He has been to 'Frisco before.

On Monday morning last I went to work putting in pieces around the truss of the lower-topsail yard. As I got more accustomed to working aloft I preferred it to being on deck. I finished the trusses on Tuesday, at two bells. On Wednesday I was at work on deck. The captain, looking aloft, didn't see me up there. Immediately the cry was "Lay aft Carpenter; Carpenter why don't you finish that truss?" To which I replied, "It was all done last night, Sir." He would not believe it without going and looking for himself, after which he took himself out of the way pretty quick.

I thought that I had been a long time occupied with the job, for afterwards Charley and I sat down in the top and watched a brig for two hours, which hove in sight that Tuesday morning. She didn't come near enough to speak to us.

We are, today, in Latitude 15°2'N, and making very slow progress for the Line. The wind still continues ahead, but for the last three days we have had a strong breeze which the second mate thinks will run us into the Trades [N. East], and I hope by next Sunday to have crossed the Line.

I am now at work smoothing up the panels of the bulkheads all over the ship. The time passes away much quicker on the sea than it does on land. I can hardly realize that I have been away from home one month [one-fourth of the voyage, I hope] and five weeks next Wednesday.

The ship is very quiet today, not hardly a sound to be heard except the splashing of the sea against the ship's side, and the striking of the bell as the half-hours are struck.

I am quite intimate with the second and third mates, but the first mate isn't just my style; he thinks too much of himself.

It makes me laugh to hear the captain and first mate advance their ideas as to improvements in the carpentering of the ship—such suggestions, that were the ship mine, I could not be hired to permit.

The crew are all busy scraping the paint off the inside of the ship with their knives. They care nothing about the vessel, they only want to kill time. If they were not watched they would scrape a hole through the side. You can tell how bare wood appears scraped against the grain with a knife.

The mizzen-topsail was reefed last night.

I think, upon the whole, that I feel as well today as I have at any time yet, and all I wish is to get to 'Frisco and hear good news for me [that] has come across the deep blue sea, and then I shall be all right.

I took a look at all of the daguerreotypes today. I have dreamt a curious dream several times, and that is that I did not come in this ship, and that I regretted it very much.

In the evenings I lie back on the spare spars and have a smoke from a meershaum worth, I judge, about $11.00; it belongs to one of the boys. I generally go without a cap, so that my head is becoming as hard as a brick. After hours I usually smoke until I become tired, and then turn in about half-past eight. I turn out at half-past five, breakfast at seven thirty, dine at twelve, and take supper at half-past five.

I suppose you are having very pleasant weather at home this month. This is a curious place, for squalls come up very quick. The heavens open and let the water drop.

I think if I were at home today I could drink a good . . . . . stirred up with a studding-sail boom.[1] I am as well today as ever I was in my life, and hope you are all the same at home.

As I have a good supply of clothing, I shall look out somewhat for the stowaway boys when we get off the Cape. One of these boys does my washing very well. I smoked one of Ned's cigars after dinner; it makes one's mouth pucker up a little.

I can guess pretty nearly what most of the Hancock Associates are doing, and also what they were doing Saturday night; when Saturday night comes around I always think of what the boys are about. I suppose they often wonder what I am about myself.

For my own part I think every man ought to go to sea for one cruise, at least, if for no other reason than to learn certain lessons he cannot be taught ashore. Even if a short cruise, it would be better than none.

I shall have a smoke, read the paper, and by that time supper will be ready.

Sunday, September 23rd, 1860.

I arose this morning and took my usual sea bath which, by the way, is decidedly refreshing in this latitude. The day is very pleasant but quite warm. One thinks nothing of perspiring here, for it drops from him as though he had been overboard.

The wind has continued to be ahead ever since we started, even up to the time of my commencing to write, when the second mate cried out, "Square the yards, and rig out the fore-topmast studding-sail boom."

We are today in Latitude 9°50'N, which is yet some distance from the Line, and the general conversation is that if we are going to have such luck as this all hands will have the scurvy, and be put on an allowance of water.

---

1   All ellipses in the journal text appear in the original typescript.

The universal impression is that it will be six weeks yet before we near the Cape; this would make it twelve weeks from Boston, under which circumstances we should be twelve weeks on the other ocean, making in all a six month's passage.

Last Friday we had what I have always wished to see—a gale of wind at sea. It commenced to blow early in the morning. I turned out at the cry "All hands to shorten sail" while the orders issued rapidly: "Haul down the jib-topsail, furl the topgallant sails, haul down the main-topmast-staysail, furl the outer jib, reef the mizzen-topsail, reef the fore- and main-topsails, &c." I had only my oil-jacket and sou'wester; but oil clothes were not of any account, for the rain was falling in torrents and the sea making a complete breach over the ship. The captain was crying out on the poop-deck, a perfect maniac, while the mates were running fore and aft upon the deck. We nearly lost two men who were on the jib-boom, the whole fore part of the ship going out of sight at every jump. While I was looking forward I saw something coming toward me, which proved to be a man just coming in from the jib-boom, a sea having struck him as he came over the bow, washing him almost over the forecastle deck. I found it about as much as an inexperienced hand could do to keep himself from standing on his head.

While I was standing to the weather main-topsail reef-tackle, a sea came aboard amidships which landed the sailmaker, who had been biting his finger nails, some of the boys, and myself, in the lee scuppers, on our backs. When I got up I could hardly see a thing for some time, the water flying in all directions and up to one's knees on the deck amidships. During this time I was not frightened at all, there was so much excitement. All hands, myself included, laughed to see the captain dance; it was as good as a play and I think the day passed away as quickly as any yet. The description that I would give of a gale of wind at sea is, in effect, the same as a fire on land; everybody full of life and excitement. It changes the dull monotony of the sea.

During the gale all hands were called four times to shorten sail. Early in the morning the jib blew into shoe-strings, with the noise of a gun. In the afternoon we wore ship, and soon after wearing ship the mizzen-topsail blew clear out of the bolt rope, parting the rope at the same time. The mainsail, which had been kept on her all this time, now commenced to show signs of weakness. The cry then was "Reef the mainsail." I started this time with the rest. The first mate looked around as I was getting into the rigging and said, "Carpenter, I don't want you or any of those boys, to go aloft today," but for my own part, I would rather have been aloft than on deck, for everything was floating about there. I considered it safer aloft than on deck, and besides, I was determined that they should see that I was not afraid to go. I had learned something from the sailmaker the first time he went aloft. He was frightened and made an awful fuss, and I caught the first and second mates looking up and laughing at him. He tried it several times before he got up. From this I made up my mind that the first time I had to go aloft they should have no reason to laugh at me.

Whenever there was a job for me aloft I always jumped into the rigging as quick as possible; and by this, I think, I got rid of going aloft on a good many occasions. I had a job, a short while ago, to slew the bands of the mizzen-topgallant sail and topsail yards. I went aloft with a large wrench hanging around my neck, while one of the men brought up my maul. During the time I was at work the ship was rolling heavily. The mate sung out, "Look out for yourself, carpenter, on that topgallant yard." That made the old captain look up, for I was at work over his head. There was not the least thing to hold onto and work, so I glued myself to the yard with my legs, and in that way managed to finish the job before I came down. The sun was hot, and the perspiration ran off of me so that I could hardly see out of my eyes.

During the gale that we had the dog came out of the fore-topmast head and, falling through the mainsail, went over the lee side. I was looking out of my room door at the time.

Our room, at this time, presented a terrible appearance, dishes, clothes, and everything else were piled up in one complete mass. The men all said it to be what is called a cyclone. It commenced to moderate that night, and by the next morning it was a calm but rainy afternoon. After the sun came out I managed to dry some of my things.

Seamen furling canvas sails on the yards of a square-rigged ship. Note the lack of backropes or safety harnesses. (Photograph courtesy of the Naval History and Heritage Command, Washington Navy Yard, Washington, D.C.)

I overhauled my chest today, and gave my things a good airing.

On Saturday morning it was found that the main-topsail yard could not be hoisted. The captain sang out for me to go aloft and see what was the matter. I sped aloft and found that the dog was out, and that the chain was grinding against the lee side of the mast. I came down from above, but the captain did not talk as knowing as usual when he wants a ten-penny nail driven. Instead, however, he said "Carpenter, what shall we do? Do you think you can fix it?" I told him "Yes," for I had made up my mind what was necessary before I came down. He said then go to work and fix it as soon as possible. I went forward and found an old dog that would answer the purpose very well. I took it aloft and fitted it in, and in a half of an hour the topsail was hoisted.

I bought a suit of dungaree clothes of the first mate and gave them to Cate.[2] I did not tell him that I had bought them for him, for he is one who would make himself too familiar. I could not bear to see a Charlestown boy want for anything. He is becoming quite smart, and goes aloft with ease.

At this very minute a sail has hove in sight, and next Sunday I will tell you about her.

This sail proved to be a ship homeward bound. Our captain ran up his signals, but from some cause or other the vessel did not respond.

It is a splendid evening, and I walked the deck with the second mate and Charles until ten o'clock.

Sunday, Sept. 30th, 1860.

The weather is not quite so pleasant today as on the previous Sabbath, it being warm but cloudy.

I took my usual sea bath this morning, aired my bed clothes and clothes in my chest, shaved myself, and went through the usual routine of rigging up.

---

2   Illegible in the original manuscript, this name is likely Andrew J. Cate, who brought only the clothes he wore and was the only boy on board from Charlestown.

Last Monday I had a growl with the mate who, I thought, was putting on airs. He is a man who thinks some of himself, but is very much afraid of the captain, so that when he gives me a job on his own responsibility he is never easy until it is finished.

He imagines he knows all about carpentering, and wants his work done in that manner. He has had some horrible looking battens made and will not allow them to be bettered.

This morning I was making a stand to go under the sheet when he told me that I ought to have more sense than to get so much work in it. That started me, and I replied that he can not be suited. This started the music. I let him know, and the captain too, that they had not a flunky to deal with. While this was going on Sam Grover, a young sailor from Portsmouth, cousin to Sid Basin, was having a row on deck forward.

I tell you what it is, fun has just commenced aboard this vessel, and before she reaches San Francisco there will be hard knocks all around. For my part I hope there will be. I think a good knock-down would make Mr. Mate more civil to me. There are four or five men in the forecastle, regular bruisers, who have been mates themselves, and don't seem to care whether school keeps or not.

The mate isn't willing to have the men talk with one another during their watch, and also insists that they should not sing at all, but they do it and that arouses him. I have always noticed that he takes good care as to where he blows. He likes to get hold of a boy and make him jump around.

During the last part of the week he has been quite civil to all hands. I suppose he has found out that he could not make the cock crow at all. I can tell him one thing, that if he ever puts his hands on me I carry something with me which will wake up his ideas. If a man is going to sea he might as well be a man as to be a coward, it pays better.

The Americans aboard the ship stand no nonsense, the foreigners only are knocked about.

Yesterday Bill Robinson, a Providence Gaspee 9 boy, had set to with the 3rd mate. I happened to be forward at the time so that I saw the whole of it. Bill soon cooled him off. It just suited me—anything for a change.

The 3rd mate told Bill to stop, but Bill told him he could not stand it, and kept on singing.

I guess they expect fun aboard. The 2nd mate asked me, the other day, if I had a revolver. This ship has had an awful mutiny aboard of her once, the scars of which she carries to this day.

On Tuesday we had another blow, which gave the ship a good shaking. When the wind blows she is just like a willow basket. This blow happened to be a fair wind, but the captain would not carry any sail on her. As soon as it begins to freshen he takes in sail and lets the ship bob about. I have not yet seen her do over eleven knots.

This day one of the pumps gave out, which made a nasty job for me. I went out to work and fixed it; it was rainy all the time and the water was flying clear across the deck.

We had to pump ship every hour and, towards the last, every half hour. I sounded the pumps at one time and found that we had made 17 inches in thirty minutes, so we immediately rigged some ropes to the pump handles [so] that the whole watch could work. They made the pumps fly.

The crew are very suspicious of the vessel, and wish to know how much water every time she is sounded. The next day the captain ordered me to sound the pumps no more. I suppose he did not wish them to know the quantity of water the ship made, so it now falls upon the mate to make the soundings.

The next day there was plenty of work for the carpenter. I rigged a stage over the bow [a piece of board about five feet long]. Charles Howard and I went down on it with oakum, mallet and irons, and found her very much opened in the wood ends on the port bow as far down as we could get; in one butt I drove three threads of oakum. I caulked the seam up and down, and then pitched it with a mop that I had made.

I must tell you of a few inconveniences I experienced in doing this job. There was not much sea at the time, but considerable swell. When I was on the stage I would go down, at times clear under, and come up wet as a drowned rat. Charles sat on the stage with his arms around the ropes, and at every sea which came he would get hold of me, crying "Look out for yourself, carpenter; if she takes me, she must take both of us." Charlie has been fishing for three years, and knows a shark when he sees it. I was driving away, with my legs in the water up to my knees, when all at once he cried "For God's sake jump for your life," which you can bet I did. None too soon, for lo and behold a large shark sped by. The job was then about half finished; but Charlie kept a good lookout, and thus enabled me to finish my task without much trouble, except getting completely drenched. All that I had on was an undershirt and a pair of duck pants, without either cap or shoes.

After I had finished this job the mate discovered trouble under the counter. I put a plank over the stern, nearly down to the water's edge, the mate promptly got down, but a good sea coming he jumped up as soon as he could, saying, "Go down, Carpenter, and see what the trouble is." I went down, and found the covering board to the cross seam was completely torn off, the lead over the seam nearly gone. This time it was impossible to sit on the stage, so they made a bowline fast under my arms, and lowered me. It took me nearly two hours to nail that lead on, for sometimes when she dipped aft I would be unable to see a thing for a minute or so. I would go completely out of sight, and when I did come up, I was as liable to be under the plank as on top of it. Jack Collins, who had been a mate on another ship at one time, and who had taken a liking to me, was tending the line. He often said "Remember Phil, one hand for yourself."

But this was not the only inconvenience under which I labored, for just to the windward a large shovel-nose shark about 14 feet long was playing up and down. A man stood on the rail watching him, and when the shark came toward the stern he would sing out "Look out for yourself." But I finished the piece of work at one job, and didn't leave it until I had accomplished it. When I came on deck the boys said, "We are glad you are done with that job. We don't like the looks of that shark."

The next day I was quite sore from the severe thump which I had suffered through the sea's throwing me against the ship's side.

Yesterday, I had two battens to make for the spanker gaff. After I had finished them, knowing that the captain would not lower the gaff without growling, Charley and I went up to put them on. As they were for the topping-lift you can imagine there was not the least thing upon which to sit, particularly as the gaff being peaked added the awkwardness of the situation. I held the pieces in place. I expected every minute to see him go off.

We meet a vessel nearly every day now, and today we have seen two.

The weather is so hot in this latitude that I wear nothing but an undershirt, duck pants, and slippers. Today we are in latitude 5°43'N, with a head wind. We have not had more than 3 hours fair wind since we started. At home, I suppose you think that I am in cold weather today, but I can tell you it is the reverse. I could no more put my bare foot on the deck than on a hot stone. My face, neck, arms and hands are as dark a brown as you would wish to see, and it seems almost impossible that my face was ever white.

I am still at work smoothing up the panels, a job one would despise on shore.

I must stop here; the captain is singing out for all hands to about ship.

In tacking ship I always go aft to overhaul the spanker sheet, haul taut the lee topping-lift and look out for the vangs; then reeve off the cross-jack sheet; by that time the ship is about.

Sunday, October 7th, 1860.

Today we are in the latitude 5°41'S, having had the south-east trade winds since Thursday; then we were in latitude 1°47'S.

From Sunday until Thursday, the heat was almost insufferable, there was hardly a breath of air, but today the weather is splendid.

We have the trade winds so strong that we do not carry sky sails at night; that is, this captain does not.

I took my usual sea bath this morning, aired my bed clothes, and went through the usual routine.

Throughout the day the weather is comfortable and warm, at night it is a little chilly.

The boys are beginning to talk about their thick clothes. Tonight is a beautiful one, and to a person inclined to stargazing it presents a favorable opportunity, the sky being entirely free of clouds or haze.

Yesterday, we made a sail directly ahead. At first we thought she was coming toward us, but it afterwards proved that we [were] going the same way. Toward night we were abreast of her, a little to the leeward. The captain signaled her. She proved to be a clipper bark from New York on her way to Valparaiso. At sundown that night she was hull down. At this very minute the second mate has come up to where I am sitting, and has pointed out to me a large ship running before the wind off our weather side. She is probably homeward bound.

This morning, about seven bells, Charles Howard sang out "Sail-ho off the main-skysail yard."

This afternoon we had a slight squall and carried away the fore-skysail backstay, and came very near losing the skysail mast.

I had a job, on Friday, to shift the copper on the main yard lower down so that the stays would not chafe the yard. The captain first asked me if I thought I could do it. He told me not to lose a nail, but you can bet I didn't tell him every time I dropped one. Imagine a person sitting on the foot ropes of a yard, with the ship rolling, copper nails, a sheet of copper, and coppering hammer in one's hands. How many hands would one be supposed to have left to keep from dropping nails? I had about four sheets of copper to alter on each yardarm. Charles was with me for a part of the time. When we were together, especially aloft, we generally make good weather of it and talk over a few of our private affairs.

I consider it quite a treat to get aloft, for on deck there is nothing but hollering and bellowing all the time.

On Friday morning I had a job, before breakfast, to go aloft and slew the truss on the fore-topgallant yard. It was blowing quite freshly at the time, and two men went up to help me. After I had got the truss fixed we were looking about when Bill Robinson said to me, "What do you suppose your mother would say if she could see you now?"

Most of the crew think that I have been to sea before.

Charles was on the fore-skysail yard all of his Saturday afternoon watch looking out for breakers. The captain supposes we are near the Rocas Islands as we saw a large number of birds toward night called boobies.

This morning we were off Cape Saint Rocque, but we saw neither the Cape or the islands.

These islands are small and in the middle of the ocean; very low down and uninhabited.

You may think it curious that I give the latitude and not the longitude. The fact is, as we have a good quadrant, the boys usually get the latitude, and while we have quite a number of books on navigation we haven't the time such as would be exact enough for the longitude, that being in the hands of the mate. The boys have made considerable progress in navigation, and often take the latitude the same as the mate.

I could easily get the longitude were I to ask the mate, but I do not like him well enough to speak to him unless it is absolutely necessary. He is what I call a regular "New York blower" and one who would starve on shore for want of ability to earn his bread.

This morning the captain's dog died, and you can imagine the rejoicing amongst the boys.

The captain was, no doubt, more grieved at that loss than he would have been had he lost one of the crew, or even his carpenter.

I rather think he believes that I have traveled considerably, for he never gets much to windward of me when he begins to blow.

The subject of general conversation now is "when are we going to reach 'Frisco; and what will we do when we get there?" I have but little to say myself, but sit and hear what the rest have to say on the subject. I talk over my plans to the boys only.

I frequently have arguments with Springfield John, who is nicknamed "Longfellow" by the third mate owing to his being the tallest person on board the ship. Notwithstanding his size, John was shipped as a boy.

You would laugh could you hear the mate singing out, "Lay aft boy John." Naturally, one would expect to see a boy, but instead one sees a person tumbling along large enough to eat hay.

The sailmaker sleeps directly under John, and often have I seen the sailmaker tumble out of his berth and on to the floor singing out, "Look out! You will be down through here. Do you want to kill a fellow? I will be hanged if I will sleep any longer under such a big ghost as you."

The boys often tattoo each other's arms, but I have not got salt enough for that yet.

I meant to have told you upon what it is that I argue with "Longfellow." It is this: he is what one calls a "greeny," and of course he thinks that it is everything to go to sea. But I tell him often, in the excitement of the argument, that I should be ashamed to acknowledge that I had been to sea and not [wish to be] associated with sailors, men among whom one finds about as little manliness as among dogs. The only manliness they manifest is fighting canvas in a gale of wind.

I suppose that there is plenty of excitement in Boston at present, in regard to elections.

I always thinks of the monthly meeting which the boys have at home and especially on Saturday nights. It would be unnecessary to say how often I think of home and of each and every one of my acquaintances.

Oh, Charlestown girls, if you could but know the troubles and trials the poor sailor has to undergo you would think more of him than you ever did before. The sailor is out in storm and tempest, while the land-lubber lies down below.

I would also mention that I stopped the leak, so that in a head sea we only have to use the pumps twice a day.

I had the stern pump to fix last week; it is a nasty old concern, and all one can do is to patch it up for a week at a time.

At present the other pumps are in good condition.

The ventilators aft were all worn out with rust. The captain asked me to cut off 2 inches all around, and put paint on each. It was what I call a job for either a tin-plate or sheet-iron worker's job, but the captain was satisfied with it when I had finished.

Sunday, October 14th, 1860.

This is the ninth Sunday on board the "Dashing Wave," and I am in hopes that I can truly call it one half of the passage, although we are not so far south as I would wish we were.

We are, this day, in latitude 18°54'S, having run south since last Sunday thirteen degrees. The first part of the week we had the wind fair, and with studding sails set fore and aft ran nearly the whole of thirteen degrees in the first four days; the rest of the week, and till Saturday, was quite calm. Saturday afternoon, however, a good breeze sprang up and has continued ever since.

The weather was about as warm on Friday as I have yet seen it. This place is said to be the hottest place in the world on a calm day.

I commenced the week by putting a handle on the cook's frying-pan. It was a cast iron affair, and the handle had become broken off. I drilled a hole through the handle and the pan, and then clinched them together.

I also worked the moulding of the plank-sheer over anew, fore and aft.

I had a job to fix one of her stern planks that had become started to such an extent that by going down the after hatch you could look outside.

I am now at work fishing the main-topgallant yard. The yard is sprung so badly in the slings that when the studding-sails were set it made it gap open quite wide.

I sawed out some oak fishes, but after I had them most done, the captain concluded that he would have them made of yellow pine, simply because he wished to save the oak. There are, on board, two or three yellow pine boards, and one five-inch plank. The boards are only one inch thick, consequently, I have had to saw the fishes out of the plank. I got three in all, about five feet long.

The captain would not think of sending down the yard, so of course it had to be done aloft. Sprung as it was, in the slings, you may know what a bad place it was to fit the fishes over the bends of the yard and around the truss; besides, the jack-stay came directly in the way.

The mate told me that the yard ought to be sent down.

All of the stock had to be hoisted up, as well as the tools, etc., and with all these things up there you can appreciate how little room there was left a man in which to work.

I think the first blow we have will carry away that yard. The captain complained that I was making it too strong, and before I had finished it, or rather fairly commenced on it, he came forward and wished to know if I had not finished it. I just looked at him for about half a minute.

This ship is said by all to be the meanest ship that sails out of Boston; she has neither screws, nails, nor stock enough for a canal-boat.

The captain does not allow me time to clean my tools or wash my clothes; and thus far, every Saturday afternoon, either the mate or himself, make it a point to have something for me to do which will last until night, so that I shall not be unemployed.

Whatever I am detailed to do, the mate makes a particular point of telling me that "The captain is in a hurry for it."

I have worked every day, save one, and that was the day of the gale, since I have been aboard this ship. But I take good care not to hurt myself in this way, finding out that they are so anxious to build a new ship on their passage, and out of nothing.

They seem to have no respect for my tools at all, and want me to work in old barrel staves and fish boxes, but they can't play any of those tricks on me. As soon as their backs are turned I seize upon one or two of the ship's tools, and with these I do such rough and tumble work as cutting off board nails and pieces of coal dust. Thus far my tools have been kept in perfect order, and are as good as when I started. But my chest is rather dirty looking as we use it for a table. I am bound to look out well for everything that belongs to me; and have been aboard this craft long enough to have learned all the dodges. I hardly believe the mate holds more trumps than I. If the mate hangs around me to work me up in to his watch, you can bet I play him a little "navy yard" in the captain's watch, and by this means I get even with the mate and am not all tired out when night comes.

You would be surprised to see how anxious they are to have a man earn his money by work. They have kept the crew busy pounding iron rust and scraping paint off the inside of her, leaving the wood bare. You can picture to yourself how the finished work must look after they have finished with it, all cut up with their jack-knives. I hope to plane the work up after them, but it does not look as well as when they commenced on it. If this were my ship I would sue the captain and mate for damages. I don't think the captain is so much to blame as the mate, who puts him up to it.

A week ago tonight I was called up twice to tack ship. I did not mind it much myself, as I had had a nap during the afternoon, but the sailmaker, the lazy pimp, made more noise than a bull. He is very much afraid that he will not get sleep enough. He sleeps almost as much again as I do, and I have plenty, so you can imagine how much rest he has.

It would make you laugh to see our room when all hands are called. Longfellow and the sailmaker are like two crazy loons, in their haste each stepping over the other, which terminates in a general "jaw" before they reach the deck. I often have a good laugh at their expense.

The food, such as it is, I can get along with; it is the same as that in the forecastle, consequently not luxurious. The only difference in our favor being that, once in a while we have a little soft bread, when there is some left over in the cabin. Three times the captain has sent in soup to the sailmaker and myself. They seem to be afraid to use their molasses; and from the economy practised; one might imagine that it cost a dollar a pint.

Both the second and third mates have told me that they thought it was the meanest ship in which they had ever sailed.

I tasted some of their cake; it was a poor specimen of molasses gingerbread.

We made a sail today, about two o'clock. She proved to be an hermaphrodite brig, running before the wind with studding sails set. She came near enough to us to see her hull quite plainly. We made signals but she did not answer.

We have had quite a fresh breeze all day. The main skysail and mainroyal bursting. We have met a few sea whales, dolphins, sharks, porpoises, flying-fish, boobies, etc.

We had a jolly row today, on account of "gouging" on the duff and molasses. The cook pitched into the sailmaker and called him everything he could. The sailmaker is the laziest man I have ever seen. Charley and I stood it as long as possible, and then decided to black-ball him. I always wait and eat my supper with Charley. Whenever the watch comes so that we three come together, Charley brings in the duff and I take the molasses. In this way we help ourselves first and get a good share, and then pass the things to the sailmaker, who dares not say a word, fearing lest something should be thrown at his head. One has always to be on hand to prevent him getting a point to windward.

Charley tried to cut off one side of the sailmaker's whiskers, the other night, but the latter turned and twisted so much that it was impossible to make a go of it.

As things are going now, I think there will be a general knock down when the ship reaches 'Frisco.

He[3] made the remark, the other day, that when he was ashore, he thought himself ignorant, but now he believes that he is the smartest man aboard. He doesn't know as much as a yellow dog.

We made the land, last Monday afternoon, off the coast of Pernambuco. As we stood in we could see the trees on the hills, small boats along the shore, and other things, distinctly. The land extended out to sea in the form of a high bluff, and looked as much like Long Island Head as anything around home with which I can compare it. It was a very welcome sight, not having seen anything of the kind for nearly two months. But when we tacked ship to stand from the land, it seemed as though we were leaving home again. It made all hands feel homesick for a short time.

I sometimes feel as though I would like to be either at home, or in 'Frisco; but when I hear the rest of them talk—men who have been to sea a number of years, I find that I did not feel half so bad as the rest of them about getting ashore.

---

3   This would have been a reference to the sailmaker, not to Charley.

Sunday, October 21st, 1860.

Owing to the weather on the 21st inst. I was unable to write, consequently this has been written on the Sunday following, i.e., the 28th inst.

I arose early in the morning, and took my usual sea bath, shaved, and went through the regular routine.

I had the long-boat to caulk during the week, and also some pieces of composition to put on the ship's rail, and the waterways around the after-house to plane over, besides numerous jobs aloft. It has become so common for the carpenter to go aloft to repair break-downs that I think no more of it than any other task.

Last Monday morning I was working upon the main-topgallant yard. It took me all the forenoon to finish it. The ship was rolling and tumbling, so that when I came down I could hardly stand up, and my head went around like a top.

We have one or two seaman who, if they were to stay aloft for an hour or two, would throw up their accounts when they came down.

This ship is a pretty bad roller, but she rolls long and low so it isn't so trying. I have seen her, when going before the wind in a strong breeze, to roll both rails under as regular as clockwork.

Last Saturday, the cook killed a pig, and there was as much talk about the killing of that animal as there would have been ashore, about where are you going to spend the Fourth of July.

After that, the crew would ask, "Well Carpenter, do you know whether or not the old captain is going to give us any of that pig, or is the mean lubber going to eat it all himself?" After they found that they were to have some, the questions then were "How are we to have it cooked? Are we to have it roasted? Is it to be a sea pie?"

I found out that we were to have a sea pie without potatoes. Of course we have had no potatoes for the past two or three weeks. The sea pie was decided upon because it goes farther.

All Sunday morning, the boys were asking, "How long before dinner time? I wonder if it will taste good?" and "I hope they will give us enough of it."

At last Sunday noon came. The wind was fresh in the morning, but fair, and with all the studding-sails set she bowled along at ten or eleven knots.

I had never eaten sea pie but was as anxious to taste it as the rest, although I asked no questions, preferring to keep my greenness to myself. While I held my peace, Springfield John was asking all kinds of questions of the men—what was it made of, and if they ate molasses on it, as he had an awful sweet tooth.

We had just commenced to eat dinner, and were well under way and into the pie, when all at once I heard something go smash, and, on looking out the door, saw the studding-booms, blocks, rigging, sails, etc., flying in every direction, while the ship was jammed aback and making sternway. The second mate fled by the door at the same moment, and sang out with a yell, "Come out of there, everyone of you." The rain was pouring down in barrelfuls all the time. One needs no calling at such times. I was putting on my oil-clothes—which by the way are very good ones and shed the water well—and when I reached the deck found that the ship was beginning to swing off a little so that things appeared a little easier. But you can imagine that there was plenty of work to be done, studding-sails to be taken in, and sails to furl and reef as quick as possible. The wind freshened to a gale, so that in an hour's time we had the vessel under close-reefed topsails fore and aft. All hands were aloft except the officers. The main-topgallant-studding sail tack got afoul the main-yard in overhauling. The mate sang out for the sailmaker to go aloft and clear it; but the sailmaker told him he could not get out there. The cry then was "Lay aft the carpenter." The carpenter went aft and the mate said, "Can you clear that tack?" I replied "I will try." I went up the lee side of the rigging as it was the handiest. The sail had not then been furled, but was only clewed up on the yard, so that it left the sheets and clews flying in all directions. I had gotten part of the way up the rigging when the sail gave me two or three good raps across the head, but I kept on, and managed to clear the tack before I came down.

As I have said before, I would rather be aloft than on deck because above the men are away from the officers, and while the smartest men haul out the earings, you are laughing at the captain to see him dance and sing. The last thing one thinks of is about falling, or anything of that kind. There are always plenty of fun and jokes on a yard; even in the darkest nights you will hear the boys on the end of the yard sing out "Light to that sail, you lubbers you, are you going to keep us up here all night?" then you will hear each one make a different reply, which adds considerably to the excitement.

When the gale struck us, I was about to tell you what a sea pie is, and of what it is made. The recipe is this: All the old pieces of the pig that the captain can't eat, pieces of dough as large as your fist and as heavy as lead, as much water as will make it thin enough to swallow by giving your teeth a good greasing. Add pepper and salt to suit convenience of cook's hand, depending upon whether it be large or otherwise. Put in a pan and place in an oven and let it stay until eight bells. As long as it stays in until eight bells it makes no difference whether there has been a fire in the stove or not, at that time it is ready for the mariners.

During this gale we lost none of our sails, but some of them received a pretty good shaking.

We have taken the oldest sails off and bent on the new ones so that we might round the Cape in better condition. Today I got completely wet through as she took one or two good seas aboard, which, when they landed on top of my head, made my sou'wester look like an umbrella turned inside out. You can imagine how one would feel, wet through and cold, your dinner cold, and no fire at which to warm up.

We have seen plenty of Cape pigeons, albatrosses, this week. The pigeons often fly on deck and can't get off until one lifts them up. They are very pretty birds, and fly something like our own domestic pigeons at home. They fly in large numbers, constantly about the ship.

Naturally, after a blow, there is plenty of work for the carpenter, both aloft and on deck.

I had nearly forgotten to tell you how the sea-pie tasted. It proved very palatable, and tasted well when it was hot, particularly when I had not tasted fresh meat for 70 days.

It comes rather hard to smell the fresh pork and the potatoes frying for the captain, and to think that one can't have any.

[Oh, topsail sheets and clew-lines too, around my head the buntlines flew].

We could not get the sun today, but supposed ourselves to be about off the river Rio de la Plata. The wind was blowing a gale such as they call a "pampero" in this part of the world.

The men say that from latitude 35°S to the Cape, there is to be had as bad weather as anywhere, and it is just here where it blows when it takes a notion.

We had some hail before night, but about seven o'clock it cleared off splendidly, but the wind was still ahead.

Sunday, October 28th, 1860.

This is a splendid morning, but about as cold as it could be at home at this time of the year.

I arose at five o'clock, my usual hour for rising, washed myself, shaved, and put on my thick flannels and drawers, [blue flannel shirt] boots, etc.

I could not stand my usual sea bath this morning, although some of them wished the fun of throwing water on me. I managed, nevertheless, to wash myself almost all over.

There is hardly any wind this morning, although there has been enough during the past week. It has been decidedly cold during most of the week; so cold, in fact, that we have been obliged to keep our room closed up to keep the wind and rain out.

The mate does not like to have us keep the door closed in the day time, for he cannot see what is going on; but he is not old enough yet to hold trumps, especially against one of the "H. Associates."

I have been at work aloft nearly all week [on the] main yard, topgallant yard, and main-top cross-trees. I have scarphed two studding-sail yards and hooped them. I had to make the hoops, as the ship had no spare ones.

You can imagine that it is pretty hard times to work either on deck or aloft, as we have a deal of rough weather. I managed, or rather had to work, with the exception of Thursday, every day last week; on that day it was impossible, being the worst we have yet had. It commenced to blow early in the morning, the ship running before the wind, but about nine o'clock, the wind hauled ahead and blew a perfect gale, the rain, sleet, and salt water flying in all directions. "All hand to shorten sail" was then the cry. We came near losing the fore-topmast staysail, the downhaul having parted, but after cutting the halliards and pulling away for half an hour we managed to get it down without tearing it. The fore topsail yard became caught in running down, which made a long delay; and by the time we were ready to clew up the foresail it took all hands to haul up the buntlines, clew-lines, etc. We also furled the mainsail and cross-jack, and set the main-spanker and the storm trysail.

There was more sea running than I had seen before; and she was taking it over the bow, stern, and waist—whole seas at a time, which made the basket squeal aloud.

The men did nothing all day but walk the deck and thrash themselves to keep warm.

After I had finished pulling and hauling, the mate set me to work in my room making plugs for the log-line; an interesting job when one could not sit on the chests without holding on, and doubly trying to stand up. The mate seems to be very much afraid that I shall not earn my salt junk.

At noon we had the ship under topsails. When she went down into the hollow of a sea it would seem as though she would never come up again, and when she did rise she would shake her sides and settle down again with plenty of water flying fore and aft.

The captain was as crazy today as ever before, and afforded laughing-stock for the men.

On Friday we had a good breeze; on Saturday it blew a gale, but in our favor. It blew so strong that we had to take in all studding sails, furl the skysail, main, and royals fore and aft, the fore- and mizzen-skysails having been sent down on deck.

Today I have had to work at carpentering the whole time, and upon the toughest scrape I have yet. It was to make a sort of partition to go around the stove to protect the panel-work. I had to make it out of wet, nasty plank, all twisted up. I matched it as well as I could, allowing the side that went up to the panels to go rough. This job would have been nothing to do could I have made it as it ought to have been made; but to suit that old captain was the worst job. He was so afraid of his old stove that he would not have the funnel or the stove moved, so that I had to make it in pieces. I could not put it together outside as it would not go into the cabin through the doors, while in the cabin there was no spare room at all for that business, and to make matters worse the captain was in the way half the time, and the rest of the time running around like a madman. I have often thought I would like to box him up. He thought, by his talk, that all a carpenter had to do was to look at a piece of board and the thing was made. He kept blowing all the time I was at work. I stood it for some time, and then I let him know that I could talk as fast as himself, which, by the way, brought the second and the third mates out of their room.

After he had finished blowing he went off, but I fancy not much ahead of the Charlestown boy.

After I had left the cabin the mates crowded around me and wanted to know what the trouble was. The third mate said he thought surely there was going to be a fight. The captain was standing on top of the poop-deck and I was underneath when I said to the mate, "If he doesn't like my style he can get some one else when we get to 'Frisco."

Hitherto I have stuck up for the ship, and thought I should go [return?] in her, but I found that that cock wouldn't crow, so I have tacked ship and sworn by all that is good and great that the minute the ship strikes the wharf I will throw my duds ashore, and recommend, also, the owners to sue the captain and mate for scathing the ship to pieces with jack-knives.

I told the third mate, when he spoke of fighting, that I had more respect for gray hairs, but I do not care any more for him than for a straw. I do not catch it one-half as bad as the second and third mates. Even the mate sometimes falls in for his share, the captain being everlastingly bent upon blowing at them.

I have seen the captain smile only once, and then he laughed in scorn at the mate's doings. The captain is what you would call a regular growl, or a bear with a sore head. I really pity the steward, for the captain is constantly dipping into him.

The captain told the sailmaker, the other day, that he had no right to think, and made him take off his boots when he was working for fear that they would wear out the sail. He dips into the poor sailmaker like a thousand of bricks.

It may not help my case to tell that I intend to leave the ship, but certainly it cannot hurt matters, for I know the mates want me to stick by the vessel. I don't like the style.

The mate has become quite sociable since we came to an understanding, but I never say anything to him unless it is necessary. All of the men are down on him. The other night he set out to strike Sam Grover at the wheel, but at the sight of Sam's knife he cooled down, swearing, however, that he would put him through; but Sam is a tough little man and doesn't care whether school keeps or not. Sam cut off the sleeve linings of my jacket, and sewed them over again for me. And in fact I can always get the men to do anything for me, and there is nothing they like better than to help me up aloft. You would laugh to hear the questions they ask me: what I came to sea for, and if it was not a hard life, &c. When I go forward in the morning to wash, nearly everyone of them will say "Good morning Carpenter."

The sailmaker presents a good picture of hard times on a cold day. He has to work every chance he gets, although he has a good deal of spare time. He has enough work to keep him busy until he reaches 'Frisco. But as for me, I have not yet had a single spare day since we sailed. I have to clean my tools every night after I have left off work, mend my clothes on Sunday, and hire a boy to wash.

All of the men say that this is the meanest old tub that ever floated. They say they were never in a ship where the carpenter was not allowed Saturday afternoons to clean his tools; and in most vessels all day. The men say that there is not a man aboard the ship who works so many hours as I do; besides being obliged to live in a small room with four others, when the agreement was there should be only three.

The captain professes to be religious, but he is not so religious that he can sell six plugs of tobacco to the men at the rate of one dollar. The Mate hasn't many scruples about charging two dollars for a seventy-five-cent flannel shirt, five dollars for boots, and everything else in proportion. The captain did make out to open his heart and give the two stowaway boys a Guernsey frock and a pair of shoes each, and which, in all probability will be all that they will get. In spite of this they have to work as hard as anyone aboard the vessel and, no doubt, will be sent ashore at 'Frisco without a cent.

I will mention a few of the inconveniences I experienced while making a covering for the stove. While standing at the bench at work, every ten or fifteen minutes she would take a sea over the weather side and completely wet me through, besides washing my lumber and part of my tools down into the lee scuppers, keeping me busy picking them up. I had to wear oil-clothes, and when it came night, after I had been out in the cold and water all day, the captain called me aft to make a thing to hang his stockings on before I ate my supper. After I had done this I had my supper to get and all my tools to clean, so you can guess I didn't bless the captain, but as my hands are getting numb from the cold, I will stop here, until next Sunday. I am sitting in the sun and along side the hatch house on a spar writing these items, with a thick jacket on, besides numerous flannel shirts; latitude 45°S.

Sunday, November 4th, 1860.

This morning the wind was fair, but the weather rather cold. I turned out at five o'clock, got some coffee to drink, and then went forward to the forecastle deck. I went there to take a view of the island of Tierra-del-Fuego. One could then just distinguish it from a cloud. Towards nine o'clock the wind commenced to freshen, and at ten o'clock it blew a gale. I had just changed my clothes throughout, but I no sooner stepped on deck than a sea, coming on board over the weather bow, landed me on my hands and knees.

At twelve o'clock we had the ship under close-reefed topsails. We were then half way through the Straits of Le Maire. One could see the islands on each side very plainly. We kept the nearest to the island of Tierra-del-Fuego. We were within about one mile of Tierra-del-Fuego, and going along at the rate of nine knots when, quick as a flash, the ship was hard aback. It brought the captain and all hands on deck without being called.

A large wave threatening a ship rounding Cape Horn. (Photograph courtesy of the Mariners' Museum, Newport News, Virginia.)

It was a critical moment; the men looked at each other but no one said a word. I stood on top of my work bench watching her back into [toward?] the rocks. There was a heavy sea running at the time, and I knew if she continued to back much farther that one thump with her stern upon those rocks would settle her case, and we would go no farther in this ship.

The sailmaker would not come on deck, but put his hand out of the window. We had another sea pie this day—having slaughtered a pig on Saturday—and the sailmaker ate so much and in such a hurry that he had to suffer for it. I said to him, "Sailmaker, you are a gone goose, the cannibals ashore will smell your breath and know you are full of fresh pork, and they will soon pick you to pieces."

You may think it strange, but he takes everything home you tell him. And he said, "My god, I wish I had not eaten so much." I thought I might as well go ashore laughing as crying. But this was not all. We made the ship pay-off and stood along for about fifteen minutes, the wind had slackened up a little on account of getting under the land, when [all] at once she was hard aback again. This time she drifted around for about half an hour, and were fast going back where we came from. I then made up my mind that it was no joke, and that she would certainly go ashore. The land, or I should say the barren, snow-covered rocks, were not more than four or five lengths of the ship astern when the breeze came off the land fair, and we got out of that mess as soon as possible. You can imagine what kind of a place this is when I tell you that it is, I suppose, in the widest place, about thirty miles across, with high bluffs and rocks on each side. Sometimes it would blow so that we had plenty of wind with double-reefed topsails, then we had a strong fair wind, then dead ahead, and then stark calm. No living thing could be seen on the land, and nothing with life but the birds flying around, such as ducks, albatrosses, Cape-hens, &c., &c. The weather was cold enough to make me put on all my thick clothes and thick boots. One could not stay on deck long at any one time without being very cold. The snow and ice looked dreary to gaze upon. The whole affair bro't back a good many school-boy thoughts when I used to study the map of South America, and read about the land of fire and cannibals of Patagonia. Little did I then think that I should ever be so near it, and aboard of a clipper ship at that.

The second mate says he has been around here in the month of July, [that would be winter here] and it was no colder than we have it now, although we have a fair wind. I am in hopes that we shall get around the Cape without trouble. As it is very cold and my hands are numb, I cannot write much, so will mention only the most particular things.

Thursday we had the worst gale yet, and then we had the ship under a close-reefed main-topsail for twelve hours. A heavy sea came aboard while I was helping haul out the fore-topsail reef-tackle. It smashed the pig pen and knocked the spars on top of the house over to leeward. Had they come down on deck they must have killed some of us. As it was, it knocked me hard up against the water casks, and hurt my right arm so that the next morning I could hardly move it.

I have been at work all the week caulking. I caulked the forward house in several seams, and also caulked a large number on the poop-deck and the after house.

They found that business was getting so brisk that something must be done; so they set one of the seamen at work carpentering and some of the boys spinning oakum. The man who had to do the carpentering did very well considering he had to use the ship's tools. When I first commenced to caulk, the captain would not get out of my way, he was so afraid I would splinter the edge of the seams; but he finally admitted that the work was done well, and then kept out of the way. I had to heat pitch in the galley, and I was afraid that the ship in rolling about might set the vessel on fire. It came very near it several times. But the work had to be done, for the craft was leaking like a sieve, fore and aft. The captain was in an awful hurry to get the caulking done, and as he could tell when I was at work by the sound of my mallet, I guess I had to earn my money this week. The last day, which was Saturday, I had several seams to caulk, but finished the work. On Monday the captain told me to go on caulking, but I told him that I had finished. He said "Nonsense, Carpenter, you could not have done it so quickly." But he found that I had, so he grunted and started off. While I was at work caulking, the pumps became defective. The mate, seeing that I was busy, thought that he would show off a little as the captain was on deck, so he commenced to fix the pumps. I saw from the start, after one or two glances, that he was about to make an extensive job of it. He worked until he was tired, and then threw the task off and on to the third mate. At eight bells their watch was out, and they were farther behind than when they began, for the boxes would not hold water at all. The second mate coming on deck, they set him at it, but when it came time for me to stop work, they had not succeeded in fixing the pumps. During their watch they had not pumped the ship, and there must have been two feet of water in her. The lack of fixing those pumps then fell upon me, which I did not care for after they had been pounding about them all day. They had covered everything with grease, and then had tried to jam the boxes down into the pump with a small studding sail yard. I had to scrape all the grease out before I could do anything with them. It was late that night before I got those pumps to work. I was bound to have the pumps in order, for had it not been for them I should have found a watery grave before this time. As the weather is cold, and as I have not a convenient place to write, I cannot enter into all the particulars. We have met but very few vessels this week.

Sunday, November 11th, 1860.

I was in hopes, last Sunday, that we should go around the Cape without any trouble, as the wind was fair until ten o'clock. But at that hour, that night, the wind hauled ahead, and Monday morning at four o'clock the cry was "All hands to shorten sail." We got the canvas off of her about seven o'clock, at which time it blew right straight and the sea began to run very high. In a short time she shipped a sea which started all the spare spars on top of the house over to leeward, which came very near hurting one of the men who jumped into the rigging in time to save himself. It also gave the pig pen a good shaking.

I believe I mentioned that in one of the blows the fore-tack bolt drew out, which made things fly around for a short time. We have plenty of snow, rain, hail and ice, and at one time there was quite a snow-balling game forward. On Thursday, it blew as hard as ever, and in the morning it commenced to rain, which br'ght avalanches of snow and ice down from aloft. Then the men began to look cold, and everything else appeared hard.

The ship was then under enough canvas to keep her "head reaching" as it is called. In the morning, we saw a brig to windward hove to, and I can tell you it was a mournful sight. One could see her when she rose with the sea, only to lose her as she disappeared behind a wave. She seemed no more than an egg shell on the water. The next day we made a bark to leeward, with her fore topgallant mast gone; but we were not able to speak her, as it blew a gale and a heavy sea was running at the time.

I have had as much as I could do, all the time, and my tools are getting into a hard looking state, being exposed to the snow, rain, and salt water. But as the work has to be done, and I am the one to do it, there is no need of complaining. Every five minutes, either the captain or the mate is crying out, do this and do that as quick as possible. I had to leave off at this place, as the captain sang out "Call the Carpenter and the Sailmaker to shorten sail." I laid aloft to help reef the fore-topsail, the second mate being short-handed. I also carried up the earing. They never order me. This is the second time today that I have been called out; this morning it was to make sail in the mate's watch, about five o'clock.

As it is getting dark I must be as brief as possible. This has been as bad a week as most men generally see. It has blown a gale the whole time. I had to help pump every two hours, and sometimes it seemed as though the pumps would never suck. I had to wear two flannel shirts, besides two drawers and a blue shirt. In addition to these, a pair of thick mittens at all times, and my oil-clothes. My boots were of no account to keep out the water, as it was sometimes over the tops of them. In that way I had cold, wet feet for a week, turning in wet and coming out smoking. I thought my feet would freeze.

I knocked the side ports out so that the sea could make a complete breach across the ship's deck. Consequently, I had to build a platform to stand upon when we pumped the vessel. On Thursday we shipped a heavy sea about noon, which, striking a man by the name of Peterson, broke his ribs and otherwise injured him. The captain had the man taken into the cabin, where the Mate doctored him. They then carried him into the forecastle. I tell you, it was a sorrowful looking sight to see that man. It was as much as three men could do to get him along, on account of the seas which were washing across the deck.

The eye-bolt that the Spencer-gaff hooks into gave away. That made a job for me. I hunted all over the ship to find an eye-bolt, but not one could be found that was large enough; so we had to unhook the cross-jack brace, and hook the gaff in that eye-bolt. This lasted very well for a day or two, but the gale increased, and that gave away too. I thought that my hands would freeze while I was aloft getting it clear. This time I got a chain, put it around the mast, made a small chock to go up against the mast for the goose-neck to set into, and then hooked the gaff into the chain. I had a job to make a port to shift from one side to the other, to shield that part of the deck where the officer in charge walks.

While I was making this port, the vessel shipped a sea which washed everything off my bench, tools and all, and down to leeward. I heard it strike and grabbed the handle of our door in time to save myself; but I lost some of my tools their being washed overboard. The sea took a large axe and drove it with such force under a water cask that we had to hook on a chain-hook to draw it out. The water went through that passage-way between our house and the hatch-house in tons. Often we get a goodly quantity into our room, the water rising above the bottom of the door. The floor is always wet, and the water often swashes from one side to the other. I have my chest upon some pieces of board to keep it out of the water. Although the top of the house has been tight heretofore, during the gale it sprang a leak. The water ran into my berth, and some even got into my clothes chest. That made me mad, I assure you, and things had to stand around in that room for a while.

I often turned into my berth with oil-clothes on, expecting every minute to be called out to do something. Charley Howard had a pair of rubber boots, and when it was his watch below, I used to wear them, so that I kept my feet dry and warm part of the time. I don't know what I should have done without them, or how I should have stood it. Charley is a great chum of mine, and he and I always take our meals together.

Just at dusk, one night, the sea boarded us amidships and stove the galley door into fragments, knocked the cook down, and filled the galley with water. I had to board it up as night was coming on, and the next morning I turned out early and put in a door. I have had to re-hang nearly every door in the ship. I have stood and watched the cabin doors, at the top, and have seen the joint open five-eights of an inch when she rolled one way, and then bury itself a quarter of an inch in the wood when the ship rolled the other way. There is a scarph in her rail where the butt opens half an inch and then closes up tight.

We have had to wear ship several times during the gale, and once the captain was in an awful flurry, he didn't know whether to risk it or not after he had got the yards squared. But he finally sang out, after looking at the sea for some time, "Haul in the main brace." The men stood ready, but not a man spoke—they all knew it was a critical moment. The captain had no sooner gotten the words out of his mouth than he said, "My God" and jumped and held on to the keel of the boat which laid atop the house. I was watching, and saw him when he jumped, and knew that something was coming. I jumped and caught a belaying-pin, while the rest were clutching anything that came to hand. A large, heavy sea was rolling down upon us, threatening destruction to everything before it. Fortunately we did not get the whole of it, or I think it would have broken our deck in; but we got plenty of it, and some of the men received some hard knocks. It seemed as though something struck me on the head and squashed me down, a peculiar sensation.

After we got ourselves clear we looked around to see if anyone was missing, but all were there. We could get along with this if it were warm weather, but as it is, what between being almost frozen anyway and then being buried in tons of ice-cold water, it chills a man's very heart. One night I was just getting my supper when the second mate came to my door and said, "Carpenter, look at this, for you may never have another chance to see it blow like this again. I have been going to sea for ten years and never did."

One of the men had to stay in the galley to keep the things on the stove. We do not get much of anything to eat in this weather, a little boiled rice and molasses, bean soup, &c., &c., and some nights a man turns into his berth pretty hungry. The cook says he has been to sea for twenty-six years, and never before has he seen such rough weather and have it last so long. All the men say they have never before seen the sea run so high, and some of them had pretty long faces on. I know I had a rather discouraging look myself for many a day. I was on deck from five o'clock in the morning until six o'clock at night, excepting what time I could catch in which to eat my meals, and when it did come night, perhaps get called out to shorten sail.

During the gale the main-topsail got started, and the mate asked the sailmaker to go up and mend it. One would have thought he was going to be murdered, he almost cried right out, and said, "I'll never come to sea again." He looked like a drowned kitten. I had to laugh at him, he

A sailmaker at work on board the *Dashing Wave* in 1898. Note the extensive running rigging and standing rigging. (Photograph courtesy of the J. Porter Shaw Library, San Francisco Maritime National Historical Park.)

made such a fool of himself. But the mate made him go up, and sent two men to hold on to him. They kept him up there a short time and then let him come down. He was so frightened that he could do nothing, so the men fixed it themselves. When he got on deck he ran around shaking his hands like a boy. All hands had a good laugh at him.

During the gale the chocks in which the steering apparatus rests gave way. I thought the captain would go crazy before I could get my tools out of my chest; he sang out for me twice, and then sent the second mate after me. Taking it altogether, I was not gone more than five minutes at the mast. I fastened it with spikes so that it was secure. I have considerable trouble with the pumps. When the pumps are worked the men shake them all to pieces. I had to pack the pumps with some pieces of blanket which the captain had. All the watch is kept steady at work pumping.

Although I have never been to sea before, I do not see but that I stand it as well as any of the others. One thing is certain, I can eat as much salt beef and stand the cold as well, if not better than most of them, whatever trouble I have to go through. I find that I am getting about as fat as is convenient for me to carry around. The second mate said, "Carpenter, how much did you weigh when you came aboard the ship?" I told him one hundred and forty-five pounds, and he said, "You weigh now between one hundred and sixty-five and one hundred and seventy." I guess he did not come far out of the way, for I cannot begin to button my clothes around me, and I tear off buttons as fast as I put them on. I tear my clothes all to pieces. I have burst all the buttons off that jacket that used to belong to father; the cap that I wore at home I cannot get on top of my head, so that I had to cut it open behind to wear it at all. One of the boys in the room, said at supper, the other night, "Look at the Carpenter, he has got two chins."

On account of getting so fleshy I find a good deal of trouble about getting on my clothes, and as for pants, I had to trade a pair of mine off with one of the boys who had a pair too large for him. In this way I manage it very well, for in warm weather my overalls, which used to go over my pants, will answer, although they are a tight fit without them. I am very sorry that I did not bring more bed clothes, as I do not sleep over and above warm. That quilt that mother gave me has got pretty well torn to pieces, but I think it will answer until I get to 'Frisco. I can then throw it away and will not be burdened with bed clothing. What is good for anything I think I shall give to Charley Howard, as he intends to make the cruise around in her. I think by the time we get to 'Frisco I shall have my old clothes pretty well worn out, and the same may be said of all hands.

Sunday afternoon, while furling the fore-topsail, I was on the yard close into the slings. The vessel made a back lurch, and in putting my hand back to catch myself I caught my fingers in the barrel that goes around the mast, and gave them a severe jam before I could get them out. It takes a long time for a cut or bruise to heal up in cold weather, especially aboard a ship where you have no mother to doctor it. But, nevertheless, I have been very lucky about getting hurt or having sore hands, compared with the rest. Most of the men's hands are sore and cracked open, and I often see men pulling and hauling with the blood running off their hands.

Besides the man in the forecastle with his ribs broken, there is another with his arm in a sling; and one of the boys in my room, John Warriner, has got such a sore leg that he cannot get out of his berth, which makes more work for us as we have to wait upon him and doctor his leg. The mate came in to look at it, and said it wanted a poultice on it, and told Warriner to chew up some hard bread, put it on a rag, and tie it over the sore, but we coaxed the cook to make a warm bread poultice for him, and that helped the sore right away. The other boy, Jim, who shipped on the wharf, has got a running sore on his leg as large as a half dollar. Both of them got their sores from shinning about, knocking the skin off, and getting cold in them, &c. Eating so much salt, a person's blood is not in a very good condition for healing.

As it is cold weather, one has to keep the door shut, and often I have to do some small job of carpentering in the room; that is, nothing but what they think possible to do. [Pigs might fly, but still they are very unlikely birds.] So far, I have never said "can't" to anything, and do not intend to if it is anywhere within the limits of reason. The main-topgallant yard, which I fished, stands good during this blow, and I hope it will until we get into 'Frisco.

I spoke sometime ago about shifting over and telling [intending?] to leave the ship in 'Frisco. At any rate, whether it did any good or not, I think that things have passed off more quietly with me lately; but forward, the men are getting more discontented and tired of each other. Two of the men, Harry Thompson and Hans, a Dutchman, got into a fight, and the next day Hans had the worst looking countenance on him that I have ever seen on any person before. The whole side of his face was black and blue.

As to the captain, I think sometimes he treats me well enough, when I hear him talk to his other officers. He said to the third mate, one day when we were wearing ship and the third mate was letting go the braces, "Clear out from there. I would rather have nobody than you." But I think

Heavy seas coming on board a square-rigger rounding Cape Horn. (Photograph courtesy of the Mariners' Museum, Newport News, Virginia.)

the third mate is a pretty smart fellow. The captain finds fault with the second mate in about everything he does; and it is my opinion that the first mate would not stand so much lip if he was not looking out for his own interest pretty well. I do not know what the captain would do if it were not for the mate, in a gale of wind.

Sunday, November 18th, 1860.

Today we are about three hundred miles to the westward of the Cape; but still to the southward. We are steering WNW, with reefs in our topsails. I arose at five o'clock, washed and shaved myself as well as possible, considering the weather which was rather cold and stormy; plenty of snow, hail, rain, &c. During the week we have had some pretty hard work and gales to weather. The worst of them is that they all come ahead, and then we have either to heave to or else man the pumps, for she is too weak to carry much sail, especially when there is so much sea running as one meets in these latitudes. On Monday morning we made a bark to windward of us, so near that when it lighted up we could see the men at the wheel quite plainly. She was hove to and so were we. The Lord only knows how near she had been to us during the night. As they found they could not range ahead of us they kept her away under our stern, and the weather thickening up we saw no more of her.

On Tuesday we made Cape Horn again about nine o'clock, and we passed by very near to it. It was a solemn looking sight, as the sea rolled up against it. We were then under topsails, and could lay our course just by the point. We had hardly gotten by, when the wind headed us off to the southward again; and it came on and blew about as hard as we have had it yet. Along toward night we had to heave the ship to again, and before we got everything snug I was pretty well wet through, which does not feel so good in cold weather. That night the men were almost perished, as some of them had not half clothes enough. One often saw a fellow wrapping flannel around his feet, and putting them in his boots for stockings, and most of them have no mittens. That night the mate did not bellow out to the men, but coaxed them along with cheering words. I did not go aloft that night, as I had as much as I could do on deck.

The captain was standing on the poop, and all hands were forward clewing up the foresail, when a heavy sea came aboard of us. The sailmaker was aft, lacing down a cover on the poop. The captain jumped up and down and cried out "My God, My God!" for he thought that he had lost most of his men. I did not blame him much, for the whole fore end of her went completely out of sight. When she came up and shook herself, the men were thrown around in all directions, some down in the lee scuppers and some were carried a considerable distance aft. The man at the wheel said it looked as though it went half way up her fore-mast. I made a grab at the fife-rail and held on, but was nearly drowned by the water. The captain frightened the sailmaker so that he did not get over it until the next day.

We saw a few grampuses during the week, and we have about us constantly a large number of these sea birds which pick up whatever is thrown from the ship. And often the men delight in feeding them.

The other night, Bill Robinson, from R.I., gave the Dutchman an awful beating. Robinson was at the wheel, and the Dutchman let go the spanker sheet, which came very near knocking Robinson overboard. We call all the foreigners Dutchman. Last Sunday, towards night, it came on to blow, and at six o'clock, when both watches were on deck, the captain sang out to reef the mainsail. This was a hard job, as the sail was wet and stiff. After we had gotten the reef tackles hauled out, I was making them fast and laying the ropes up on the pins. By that time the men that were able to go aloft were in the rigging. I did not care to go much, as I was getting tired, but I saw the mate looking toward me kind of wistfully, so I jumped into the rigging. The mate said, "Well done, Carpenter." We all laid up except the boy in my room, John Warriner, who, for the first time, rather hung back. The mate said "Come John, where are you?," and at that he started aloft, and came up into the top to help me and another man to haul up the studding-sail booms, so that the men could tie the reef points.

After we had them triced up, instead of going down on the futtock shrouds, we went over the fore side of the top and down on the main stay on to the yard. As we came down the third mate said, "Carpenter, you come with me; let John go on the weather side." They had got the earing hauled out, when we got on the yard, and were just commencing to tie the points. I had just got hold of a point, when, all of a sudden, I heard a crash which sent a chill through every heart on that yard. There must have been either a lull, that we heard the sound so plainly, or else it was a loud crash, for one could not hear a man speak at that time, on the yard, the wind was blowing so, but we all knew by the sound that someone had gone off the yard.

All were asking who it was that fell; but one could not find out until one got on deck where, horrible to relate, there lay the boy, John Warriner of Springfield, Mass., a mangled heap. It is supposed that, as the yard was large where he stood, he took hold of the end of the fore point and reached down under the yard to catch the other one and, in so doing, his hands, being cold, slipped off and down he went head first. He struck his head on a spare spar on deck, and his legs on the iron pump-handles which project out. He made quite a mark on the spar with his head, and his legs bent the handles down to the deck. The captain was looking out of the cabin window at the time, and saw him falling, but did not know who it was. The mate and the sailmaker picked him up after they got over their fright. When the captain came out the first word he said, so the sailmaker told me, was "Where is the Carpenter?" While I was on the yard, before I came down, I heard the men say "That was the Carpenter who fell," and many of them thought it was me until I showed myself. They took Warriner into the cabin where the Mate bled him; his heart then beat. Some of the men rubbed him and the rest did everything possible, but the blood ran from his mouth and ears in a stream. Although everything was done that could be done for him, it was of no avail, for at 9:30 o'clock that morning, the eleventh day of November, 1860, he died, having lived nearly two hours after he fell. He never uttered a word, but only groaned in falling.

Although Warriner was called a boy, he was as large as anyone on board, being six feet two inches tall. He belonged in Springfield, Mass. His father was a banker, and was aboard the ship [the day] when we sailed, and no doubt thought a great deal of his son. The father had given his son a good education. John had just finished schooling at the age of eighteen, and then his ambition was to be a sea captain, but alas for him his days are ended. The last words his father said to him, on leaving the ship when we parted with the steamer, were, "Be a good boy, John, and take care of yourself." John had the daguerrotype of all his folks in his sea-chest, and often he would take them out and say, "Carpenter, you cannot guess how their hearts will beat with joy when I get back home again." He had a father, a mother, a brother, and a sister. He had as good an outfit as any one on board.

The next day, which was rather a sorrowful one, we packed up his clothing, &c., put everything in his chest which belonged to him, washed out his clothing which he had on at the time of his death, and which were all covered with blood, and then stowed his chest down aft. He always kept a journal, even up to the day he was killed, which, no doubt, his folks will be glad to read over. He used to tell me about the letters he was going to have when we got to 'Frisco, &c., and what letters he was going to send home. He and I used to have long talks together, and he would sit for hours and listen to me tell over scrapes, and ask all kinds of questions. He, being from a back city, did not know our city ropes.

On Monday morning, I made a bier to lay him on, and the sailmaker sewed him up in his blanket, and then the men put some old iron in a bag and tied it to his feet. He laid on a platform, aft of the pumps, on which we had to stand in pumping the vessel, during the forenoon. After one o'clock, that day I laid some plank from the booby-hatch to the rail, and on this we laid him on his bier. About half-past one o'clock all hands were mustered aft into the forward cabin. The captain then read in the Bible and offered up a prayer. We then stood each side of the staging with our heads uncovered and, at a given sign, the plank was tipped up and the corpse was buried in the deep blue sea. Before we went into the cabin, we backed the mizzen topsail. When the remains of Warriner were launched into the deep, the captain felt so bad that he had to turn his back, and being nearly overcome, shed tears during prayers. One may know we all felt bad enough in our room, having had one taken from our midst so suddenly, and none of us slept the night he was killed. We often look into that berth of his, and finding it empty, the sight brings back former recollections.

We spoke the English "Roxbury Castle," this morning, going before the wind with royal studding-sails set, while we were on the wind with reefs in our topsails. On Friday, we saw a double topsail ship bound with us, which the mate thought was the "Aurora" of New York. On Saturday we took a fair wind about six o'clock, but later it blew so hard that the captain didn't dare to run her, so hauled the vessel on the wind. This seemed rather hard after we had been wishing for a fair wind so long, to have so much of it that we could not make good use of it. The captain wanted to run her bad enough, but it was of no use, she was going out of sight at every jump. I have seen her decks filled with water on the lee side as high as the pin-rail. She filled the forecastle with water twice, so full that the men's chests floated about, and the berths and so forth were wet. The sea floated everything forward aft to the cabin door. The watch below jumped out of their berths as quick as possible, they thought the ship was going down. This time I had to laugh to see all hands scampering in all directions. The captain jumped up and down on the poop, the cook crawled on top of the house and was singing out bloody murder, while the men fled up the rigging on top of the house and any other place that came handy. I was at work at the bench, and heard the sea strike forward. I jumped on top of my bench and held on to the lashings which go over the top of the hatch-house, and by the time I got on top I saw the sea coming, tons of water raking everything before it—casks, wood, lumber, buckets, &c. But the sideports being out, the ship soon cleared herself. One may know how hard she was pressed when she made nineteen inches of water in twenty minutes.

I was taking in sail and pumping the vessel all that afternoon. We kept along in this way until Sunday, the 18th, when the wind hauled ahead again, which made all hands put on long faces. But I kept up my courage, and always tried to be around when there was anything being done, reefing, furling, or making sail, for I find that at these times sailoring is thought more of than carpentering, and for my own part I prefer the former to the latter. I like to reef or furl sails when the weather is not too cold. The other day I was coming down off the crossjack yard—I had been up to help furl the sail—when the Mate said to me, "Carpenter, you know you are under no obligation to go aloft to hand sails; it belongs to the sailmaker to do that, if necessary, but I like to have you go if you will. You know you are considered as the mechanic." I told him that I would go as long as we were in cold weather and short handed.

I generally help to shift over the main-topmast-staysail before tacking ship, but it is my duty to tend only the spanker sheet. In case of a blow, the third mate and myself generally take the bonnet off the staysail. A bonnet is something one does not see often on a ship's staysail. Since John was killed, there has been an entire change on board the ship. The mate feels it the worst, for it was he who sent the boy aloft. The day John was buried, the mate cried, and when it was time to tip the plank he could not speak, but made a motion with his hands. The mate came into my room to look after John's things. The boys were in there at the time, and he talked to them like a father to his children, and said that from that day he would commence another life. I believe him to be sincere, for during the last week I have never before seen a man alter so. He always appears to be in deep thought, and always speaks pleasantly to the men. To me he is as good can be.

The second mate is a strictly religious man, but not radical. He spends hours at a time talking with the mate, and it is a common expression, "How altered is the mate." The mate let one of the stowaway boys, Charles, have John's oil-coat until we should get out of this weather, and to the boy James he lent his oil-pants, but everything else he was very particular to send home to John's friends. We all of us say, "My God, what will they [John's friends and parents] say when they overhaul his chest?" They will find there his sheath-knife and belt, his journal which he kept so regularly every day, besides numerous things which he had received aboard ship. They will also find one of my cards which I gave John. I think if I live to reach 'Frisco I shall write to his folks, to let them know that he received every attention after he was hurt, and that he was liked and respected by all as a kind friend and a true sailor. His ambition was to be a sailor, and thus he lived and died.

I often wake up in the night and look around in the room, and instead of seeing two boys sitting chatting together, there sits one alone on my chest wishing for the morning to come. If I move, the boys generally ask me if I want anything, and they always cover me over if they see the clothes getting off of me in the night. I most always turn out at twelve o'clock when the watch is relieved, have a look around and then turn in again. One thing that struck me more forcibly than the rest was the sea that we shipped. It washed a tub down to our door, and, as the ship rolled, the tub would go from our door out to the side. In that tub were John's jacket and pants, soaking the blood off. But I will say no more of this as I do not find it very agreeable, for I can pity his folks as well as though he had been my brother.

I forgot to mention that one night, while we were lying to, it was as thick as thick could be—the man on the lookout had to stand along side the foremast, the water flew so—when all at once he sang out, "Sail ho."

It gave everyone a start, for we were running down on top of a large ship, and soon would have been on top of her. We showed our lights to let her know that we saw her.

There was one day when we reefed topsails four times before night; make sail and take in sail was the order of the day, and in furling the foresail I have known men to get wet through and thro' on the yard. She is what you call a regular "Dashing Wave," truly. The captain, when it is bad weather, stands in the forward cabin and looks out of the window, and appears comical enough with his white head and white whiskers.

The boys keep the fire going in the cabin during the night, and on the stove they always keep chocolate. The Mates sometimes slip some of it into the boys' pots, and they always come and wake up the Carpenter to divide it with him. The boys and I always get along first rate for, to tell the truth, I have not as yet gotten over all my boyish tricks, and we are always up to anything for sport. But, alas, the sailmaker is forever in a row. The boys, however, don't care a farthing what he says or does.

In this country one can have what is called "long days." It is not dark until ten o'clock at night, and is daylight between two and three in the morning. But it is not often that one gets a chance to see the heavens, the weather is too boisterous. We were, today, in latitude . . . . . . , but on Monday we reached as high as 55°S. When I started from Boston, I expected to have crossed the Line on the Pacific side before this time, but as it is I have to make the best of it, as there are others who feel worse about the long passage than I do. I do not seem to care whether school keeps or not now that we have gotten around the much talked of Cape Horn and are headed north.

Cape Horn well deserves to be talked about. I was thinking about the election the other day, and was wondering who could be the President, and if he were the man for me and our family. I think of the torch-light processions, bands of music, &c., &c., that have been going on in Boston while I am on the deep contending with the storms and gales of that well known place, Cape Horn. I think of the warm coal fires by which my acquaintances can warm themselves while I have none, and am obliged to dry my wet clothes by hanging them up against the partition which comes nearest to the galley. This is the nearest that I ever come to a fire—

Green seas running the length of the deck on a ship rounding Cape Horn. (Photograph courtesy of the Mariners' Museum, Newport News, Virginia.)

the boards upon which we hang our things are about five feet from the galley stove. We call these boards our patent drying-machine. You would laugh to see it, it looks like a checker-board adorned with gloves, mittens, stockings, shirts, pants, &c., &c. It generally takes twenty-four hours to finish drying, but sometimes we do not wait for our things to dry. If they have been hanging up there that is enough, take them down and have what is called a "sailor's shirt."

Love can excuse anything, but meanness cripples even natural affection.

Sunday, November 25th, 1860.

Today, we are in latitude 49 south, longitude 83 west. The weather is getting warmer, but we still have a good deal of rain and fog; we do not see the sun, sometimes, for four or five days. It is raining very hard today, and in the forenoon we had to shorten sail. The captain called the carpenter and the sailmaker. I went through the usual routine, and had hardly finished when the captain called again. The second mate came to the door of our room and asked us to lend him a hand to get down the flying-jib. I went forward. There were only three men of the second mate's watch on deck, the rest were aloft with us. We numbered five, but the sailmaker was fit for nothing, for he hardly dared to get up on the forecastle deck, and when he did he had one hand on the downhaul and the other on the windlass brakes.

To be sure, it was not a desirable place for anyone to be when it is blowing hard and with a head sea. For about one-half of the time we were under water. But when we do go up, I like to see everyone haul and get down as soon as possible. The captain sang out to furl it. They looked at each other before they started—there were only three of them—but I said, "Go on. Let us get out of this as soon as possible. I will go out and help you." So we all started, and I assure you it is no easy road to travel to get out there. After we did get out there we bundled that canvas up in a hurry and got back on deck. I had often heard of furling flying-jibs, and now I know what it is to perfection. There is not a man on board the ship but that says he hates to go on that flying-jib boom. The men with whom I went out were as good sailors as one generally finds, but it made them hesitate. When we came in off the boom, the rest of the watch were on deck, and all of them stood looking at us while we were coming in and while we were furling the sail.

I often see the Dutchmen dodge to get clear of going out. I would not have gone out had I not liked the fellows pretty well, and have known them to be men enough to appreciate an act of that kind on one's part. I cannot exactly express it, but a person feels a peculiar sensation while in such a place. One has only a small spar to hold on to, and every time the sail flaps you get a good shake. One has a good look at the salt water and the bows of the ship as she comes thundering on, threatening destruction to everything in her way. By that job I got pretty well wet through, for I didn't put on my oil pants, but put on only my jacket, and that being loose blew out and let the water fly up my back in barrelfuls. You may know whether I have any use for oil-clothes when I tell you that my suit was double and brand new, but now they are worn threadbare and leak like a sieve. I have patched them to make them last, but by the time I get to 'Frisco they will be so fine that I shall hardly be able to see them.

Today we are 102 days out. This, according to your reckoning would make me, I suppose, within 17 days of 'Frisco, but as I reckon now, 47 at least. It is evident to me that signs of scurvy are making their appearance among the men, but as for myself, I never knew what it was to be more hearty. I have an appetite like a bear, and eat as much beef for supper as I would eat for dinner at home. The boy James has been sick this week with awful looking sores breaking out on his arms and on his legs. I hardly know what to make of them. We caught a porpoise Thursday, which weighed, I should think, 200 pounds. We had him cooked, and it tasted very well; for anything fresh or sweet we bite at like a shark. I have no doubt that when you eat your Thanksgiving dinner, which according to my reckoning comes on the 29th, that Philip will be thought of more than once.

Last Sunday night I had to go to work and get out a large chock to fit over the screw-gear of the rudder, as she was tearing everything to pieces. It was a bad job in the rain, and a gale of wind was fast coming on us. After I got it done the captain was as agreeable as I ever saw him. He did not expect to get it done so quickly, for we had to unlash spars, &c., to get the stock to make the chock of. He had the whole watch running about to help me. You can guess that things flew around for a time. He never said a word the whole time I was at work, but gave me plenty of room. Before I finished, I was well soaked through, and then I had to wipe my tools off and oil them. I found no fault because it was necessary.

This week I had two old pistols and a lock to mend; and the captain has yet a clock which will need mending soon. The pistols were loaded, and I had to draw the charges. Most of the week I have been at work making and shortening sail. The other morning there were three of us, two besides myself, trying to furl the mizzen-topsail, but could not do it until we got some help. I also made a head for the capstan, which pleased the mate very much.

The ship presents an awful sight forward. Her bulwarks are torn off and her bowsprit is all loose. Her forecastle-deck is pretty well wracked to pieces, and when she plunges into a sea she shoots the water in by barrelfuls. The butts in the deck are all open, and in the seams alongside the waterway you can drive an iron in the whole length. She has also knocked her stern mouldings off. I never should have believed she would have stood so many gales of wind. The captain is much afraid of her and heaves her to every blow that comes, because it would not take long to fill her full of water. Her cargo must be damaged, and as soon as we get into good weather I shall have plenty of caulking to do. We have seen no sails this week except our own, and those we have seen often enough. We are what one can call around Cape Horn good and clear, and I hope to be in 'Frisco soon. I have been aboard the packet long enough to know my duty, and I care but little for any of them, from the captain down to the cook who is a saucy old nigger, and for whom I bear no regard—a feeling which seems mutual. But I have stood it so long that I think I can stand it for the rest of the time easy enough.

Sunday, December 2nd, 1860.

Today we are in latitude 36 south, and about the longitude of 90 west. This has been the best day we have had for a long time, and I suppose now that I have got the best of the Boston people, for I can go about in my shirt sleeves. Until last Wednesday we had had continual gales ever since we passed the river Rio de la Plata. Last Monday we had a severe gale, and although it was a fair wind we had to heave the packet to. With this the mate found a good deal of fault, and said the captain had ought to keep her off the wind or tear her to pieces. As soon as we got a fair wind, which was a long time coming, we soon ran into warm weather which made every heart beat with joy. On Saturday we shook the reef out of the mainsail, which had been in for a long time.

On Thanksgiving day we had to work the same as any other day. That, you must know, did not suit me as well, for I have not been in the habit of working that day, and I let them know it, but it was no go. Work is what they want, but they did not make more than twice out of me. That day we had our usual rations of salt-horse, and so the day passed off very agreeably to us as we were fast getting into better weather. At night I had a general talk-over of past times at home, what the boys were doing that night and what I was doing myself a year before at home. Freeman and I went to the Howard Atheneum. I wondered if sisters and brothers collected around the dinner table, and if they gave a thought to the carpenter of the "Dashing Wave," and if little Ellen Frances ever looks up into her mother's sweet face and says, "O where is uncle Philip?" If she does, what her mother says to her is this, "He has gone to sea and has already doubled Cape Horn, and never, for once yet, has he, even while in the worst weather and under most trying circumstances, disgraced the name of Charlestown."

I suppose the talk at home is that I am about getting on the coast of California; but alas for me I am off the coast of Chile. I suppose there was a dance in Pigville, Thanksgiving eve, and no doubt some of the boys went. If they did as they usually do, they had one of Dan Ames old times. I should really like to know who is the President of the United States. It is really hard for me to be so long on the passage, because it is so much money lost.

Nevertheless, I do not feel as bad about it as a good many others aboard, for most of them are crippled in some way. We have thirteen of the best men on the list. Some of them have to work with one hand, others are lame, &c., &c., but as for me, I never was so strong before in my life. The boy James, in my room, has as sore a looking leg as I have ever seen. It is a complete scab from the knee down to the ankle. There doesn't seem to be anyone who knows what it is. But his blood is bad, and while eating so much salt provisions it will never heal up at sea. He often asks me about it, but I never say anything to discourage him, but tell him it will go away as soon as he gets ashore. The stowaway boys are well, and have more clothing now than some of the men. The boys were allowed to stay in the forecastle in the worst weather because the water which went in at the toe of their boots ran out the heel. In the dog-watch the boys come aft into the room, and as all of them are good singers I get them to sing while I lay off. I laugh to hear them tell what they are going to do when they get ashore. They say the first place they will go for will be an eating-house, [not Moses Pearson] for they believe they can eat a mince pie six months old. I have been at work during the week making belaying-pins and repairing the wreck forward which, by the way, is no small job. The captain is awfully afraid he won't get work enough done for his money. I have a jack-knife mate at work now all the time, and the sailmaker has three or four, for the sails got pretty well torn to pieces and looked more like rags than anything else. They had cheek enough to ask the man with broken ribs to come on deck to work when he is spitting blood every day. The captain made him get up and come aft to him, and when the man told the captain that he could not stoop the captain laughed at him. I pity a man who gets hurt at sea. Nearly all hands have boils. The sailmaker has a sore finger, and a boil on his wrist. Thus far I have escaped, and for that reason I find no fault with my situation when I see others working in misery. Nothing short of broken limbs is of any account here. Square the main-yard and rig out the studding-sail booms. We saw a sail to windward today—the first one for a long time.

Sunday, December 9th, 1860.

Today we are, as near as the second mate could tell, in latitude 21 degrees south and 103 degrees longitude west. We have gotten into good weather so that the men can go about on deck bare-footed. Today is rather cold on account of a strong north-east wind which prevails, though not prevalent in these latitudes. It is rather squally and cloudy, but I have never seen the ship fly as she does now. We have the wind three or four points free, with a topmast studding-sail, and that gives her all the canvas she can carry. She goes all the way from ten to fourteen knots, and for a mile astern one can see nothing but a complete foam. This ship could be made to go over fifteen knots today, but she would twist up like a basket. But as the captain thinks that good ships and good men are scarce, he is going to take care of himself and the vessel. We have had a fair wind ever since last Sunday, which enabled us to make the best week's run since I have been aboard the packet; and as we are likely to have it for the coming week I am in hopes to tell you next Sunday that we are near the Line, if not across it. We have not met any vessels this week. You may know that I am anxious to get ashore by this time, for it is quite long enough to be on the water for one trip of this length. I think that I am about as homesick now as I was when I first came out, i.e., I have felt so ever since we got the fair wind, for everybody is talking about getting in and what they are going to do. It would make you laugh to hear the sailors build castles in the air about what they are going to do when they get on shore, you will never catch them at sea again, &c., &c. Whenever there is a fair wind, they say, "We shall get there in three or four weeks," then the next day, if the wind hauls ahead, "We are going to be 200 days, and we shall all have the scurvy." You would be surprised to hear how superstitious they are. One thing is curious, and that is whenever a pig is killed we always have a gale of wind the next day. Whether there is anything in it or not, I have seen it tried four times to perfection, and never miss. Yesterday, a pig was killed, and it is blowing heavy today, although we do not mind it much because the wind is aft. There is plenty of work going on aboard this packet, and there will be until we get to 'Frisco.

The ship has to be painted all over, and her rigging fixed before she goes in, i.e., if there is time; but all hands pray that there won't be time, for it has been nothing but scrape and clean paint ever since they came aboard. The men are saucy and growly now, and I doubt if they scrape much more paint. They say that the mate does it to wear out their knives, so that they will have to buy new ones of him. You would think, to hear the captain and the mate lay out work for me, that I had a gang of carpenters aboard.

The first part of the week I was at work repairing the head, putting in new fastenings, new bulwarks, and a piece of rail which, by the way, is not a very desirable job—being obliged to get astride the bowsprit stay with the ship going nine or ten knots and lumber in your hands. They calculate, because a man has "carpenter" affixed to his name, that he comprises a lumber yard, a blacksmith's shop, and a hardware store.

On the luff of each bow, she is spread so that you can shove your hand into the butts of the forecastle deck. I wanted the captain to come forward and have a look at her before I commenced, but he wanted me to go ahead and get it done as soon as possible. He did not like the idea of going, but at last he made out to get up there one night; and when the men saw him they set up a regular laugh; which made him step aft in double-quick time. I told him that the best thing to do was to drive in some pine wedges and caulk them. He told me to go ahead and do it but not to caulk any until I had caulked the main deck. The next morning he came forward, before I had gotten my breakfast, and asked me if I had caulked the wedges. I looked at the man in astonishment. I said, "No. You told me not to do that work until I had caulked the main deck." He said, "I didn't tell you any such thing." He commenced to talk loud, and I just let him know that I had a good pair of lungs too. He went aft and got his breakfast, then came forward where I was at work saying, "Carpenter"—in quite a different voice—"I don't see how you came to understand me so?" But I would not have anything to say to him, at all.

After I had finished forward, I went aft and told him I was through. He was as smiling as a basket of chips, but he can't come the possum over me. I think he is a regular bear, the more you do for him, the more he wants and expects. Work which the mate says is done first rate and praises up of his own accord, the captain says is "done after a fashion." And I have never done a job to suit him since I have been aboard. I have the main deck to caulk, and a large number of graven-pieces to let in, doors to mend and, in front, work enough to last me back to Boston. I do not have a minute of time to myself. I hire someone to wash for me, and I mend my clothes on Sunday, or get some of the men to do it. I am not given even time to clean my tools, so I have to do it at night after I get through.

The second mate says that the captain will want us to work twenty-five hours a day if he keeps on. The men say they have been in regular Black Ball packets and did not get turned to work so early in the morning and so late at night, nor did they get beans twice and rice three times a week. But as to the grub, everybody, mates and all, find fault. For myself, I am quite surprised. I can eat as much salt-horse as anyone and, in fact, a good piece goes good. As for myself, I can get along with the grub very well, altho' the second mate says she is the meanest living ship he was ever in, and I often hear the mates talking about what they have to eat. The captain opened his heart the other day, and sent twelve pickles forward, for twenty-four men and two boys, and gave us, in our room, three. If it is good or bad living, I cannot tell, for I have never been in any other ship; but this much I know, and that is, I get about as fat on it as is convenient for me. Yesterday the mate asked me if I could go aloft, Sunday, to see what work there was to be done. But he can't play that on me. If I can't get time during the week, I can't get time Sundays. That man that broke his ribs was set to work, and not being knit, they broke apart, and so he is laid up again.

Sunday, December 16th, 1860.

Latitude, 12 miles north of the Line and near the longitude of 115 degrees east. This week we have had a fair wind, with studding-sails set all the time, and have made the best week's run of any week yet. This makes fourteen days of fair wind. It is a splendid day, the wind fair, and, as a general thing, everything fair and around in the right corner now that we are about getting in. Even the captain acts now as though he had but one row of teeth, the same as any other human being. Ever since the morning we had the blow about the deck he has been quite civil, but for this reason only: the ship is going to have some repairs made when she gets to 'Frisco, and how nice it would be for him to have me stop in the vessel and work, while if he hires other men, as I know he has got to, he will have to pay them from five to six dollars a day. This is going to bring "old Skinflint" to his senses, especially when he owns part of the packet. His meanness extends to studying economy on sailors' grub—and will also put him in mind of the carpenter he had from Boston. The carpenter that he had before me, the men tell me, could do nothing at all, and in fact he had no tools; but for all that, the captain did not want him to leave in 'Frisco. All the men forward are going to leave, and aft, the third mate and myself. I do not think the other mates would need much coaxing to go in another ship.

There is one thing I will say, and that is, I know that if I had had more to say to the captain and less to the mate I should have made considerably better weather. The mate eternally kept me agoing first on one thing, and then on another before I was done with the first, but the captain always asks me if I have got through the job. If I go aft to the captain I do not get such unreasonable jobs as I do from the mate. When I am at work for the captain the mate knows better than to meddle, and is always quite sociable to me—and mark the distinction between "Carpenter a pull there" and "Carpenter I wish you would give us a pull." The mate commenced to talk to me, the other day, like a more civilized man, and among the many things that he mentioned was that the captain was always talking about me, and had spoken as many as half a dozen times about how fat I had gotten since I sailed from Boston. There is one thing that makes the mate stare, and that is when I say, "I can just tell you one thing, I don't go to sea for a living, and it ain't for the $20 a month that I came in this packet." Then you will hear them say they wish they could get something to do ashore.

I am now at work on the ship's main-deck, new plugging it, caulking and putting in graving pieces. Since they have kept up their dignity all the passage thus far I am going to make them keep it up the rest of the way. They can't come the double over me, and if they commence talking to me about home and things in general, I go away. But, nevertheless, I like the second and third mates. The second mate is a perfect brick, and will come and talk with me all day. If the captain is along side the captain looks daggers at him. And the captain, in a gale, instead of staying on the poop where he belongs, comes down on the main deck and begins to hallo about—you can't understand a thing he says. The second mate takes no more notice of him than though he wasn't there, but keeps on about his work. The captain stays until he gets a good sea on top of him, then goes aft. I have seen all hands laughing at him as he went around scrambling on his hands and knees, singing out "Mr. Maynard." But no use, a mate feels himself insulted to have the captain come on the main-deck and give orders.

I should like to know what kind of a day you have at home, for I have gotten my mattress out and put it on my bench where I lay off and take things cool. I have plenty of cigars now, for I bought 150 nice ones from the mate for $3.00. Today Charlie and I are going to have a piece of that plum cake that sister Fannie made me, on the strength of crossing the Line; and we are going to look into that refrigerator that stood in the corner of my chest. I always remember what Fannie told me. It was this: "Remember me when you eat this cake." Thus far, although I have often thought of her, I have not had to eat cake, for every time I lift the cover of my chest, I see the word "Sister" on perforated paper. I dreamed twice in one week, just before Thanksgiving, that she was married, and it became so much impressed on my mind that I spoke about it. I suppose you have said, today, "I suppose Philip is in 'Frisco now, and the next steamer we shall hear from him" but, alas, you will be disappointed. But it will be doubly welcome when it does come, and I should like to be in the back room and hear it read. The last words that friend Frank said were, "Good bye Phil, for 120 days." The reason why I do not use more names of my friends in this journal is that if I used their names, and told all I thought about them, I could not write anything else. But rest assured that not a single friend is forgotten by me, and in due time they shall hear from me and my doings aboard the packet "Dashing Wave." A sailor's sixth commandment: "Six days shalt thou labor and do all thou art able and Sunday wash decks and scrub the cable."

On for 'Frisco.

Sunday, December 23rd, 1860.

Perhaps you may think it a little curious, in reading this journal, to see certain phrases in it such as the preceding, but I see them so well illustrated in my present position that I cannot help writing them when they come to my mind. Today, we are in latitude 16°45' north, that is, we were at eight bells. The weather is rather cloudy, but comfortable. The northeast trade winds which we took in latitude 5°N, are quite strong now, so that we often have to furl the royals. We had but few light winds on the Line, but plenty of moisture; and consequently my oil clothes are now no more account than brown paper. We keep over and above a supply of water on hand all the time, and there is scarcely water used of the tank yet, which holds 3,300 gallons. The day it rained so hard the pumps gave out, which made a wet job for me, but when it rains I cut out diamonds and belay pins in my room. You would suppose it comprised a large carpenter shop.

The captain had the top of the after house scraped off; it was a quarter of an inch thick with old green paint and full of knots. There were more knots in that deck than I ever saw before in a collection. There were some planks fifteen feet long which had five, six, and seven large knots. The sailors, in scraping, when they came to those large knots would go over them lightly, but when they came to a soft place they would scrape a hole clear through if you didn't tell them to move. They say that it makes no difference to them, they are only waiting for it to be eight bells. The captain concluded to have it planed over, the plugs dug out; and diamonds put in, besides an unmentionable number of graving pieces. He always ends off by saying he must have it done as soon as possible. I went to work and adzed it all over, which rather pleased the captain, and for the first time he spoke to me outside of business; he inquired about affairs and work at the Yard.

There were so many pieces to let in the deck that he let me have three of his best men to plane the deck and brought to sight the ship's planes. I fixed the planes and set the men to work; but it was about as much work to look after them as it would have been to do the work myself. They cussed the job, ship, captain, &c. I had many a good laugh to see them plane. They would keep one eye on the captain, and when his back was turned they would keep the plane going backwards and forwards with one hand, and not a ghost of a shaving would the plane cut. They would do that half an hour at a time. They don't care now whether school keeps or not. The mate and one of the best men had a row on deck, the other morning. Thus far I have got the deck planed, but not one-half the pieces let in yet; some planks take four pieces. The steward told me that the captain was very much pleased with the deck. As the steward stands at the table when the captain and mate eat, he hears all that is going on. I have done some painting and puttying in the cabin this week, and I mistrust that whoever goes as carpenter of the "Dashing Wave" from San Francisco, will have to plane the main-deck, fore and aft.

Extensive preparations are now being made for entering port, for you may think with a strong fair wind we could easily reach 'Frisco by next Sunday. At the same time, I give her one more Sunday for me to be aboard. Although this ship has some bad qualifications she has also some good ones. Yesterday the captain concluded to have the spare spars rolled to the side, after we have climbed over them for the last four months, forty or fifty times a day. We can now go across the deck without climbing. Many a piece of skin have I knocked off my legs falling over those spars in the night; and the ship seems like another vessel now that they are moved. The lumber that was put aboard is getting rather scarce, and she will have a new fit-out in 'Frisco. The captain was telling me about new ladders and cross-trees he is going to have made when he sails from 'Frisco. He takes me for a "greeny," I guess. If I had intended to go the passage in her, his kind of encouragement would have made me alter my mind; and I say as the men say, "If the captain don't like me, I don't like him," so there is no love lost. Sailors as a general thing, aboard this ship, think there is no such place as Hell; but think that they get punished for all their sins when they get to sea; and I must say that they are good on an agreement of that kind. Friday they call a regular "bean-day." They don't get very much to eat and always have a head wind or a gale, and more than one-half the time it comes true.

Next Thursday is Christmas at home, but I don't expect it will be all the same with me. Here the captain has too small a soul to think of Christmas. Here, in the hatch-house of the "Dashing Wave," off the coast of Mexico, I wish all of you a Merry Christmas; and God knows if I could hear it echoed back, I should hear the sound of many voices wishing me a good many returns of the day. I often think how Jimmy looked when I bade him good-bye, in Elm Street. He was sitting on top of a peddler's cart, rather a prominent position, and sister Augusta said, "I know you go for your own good, but it is such a long, long way from home." It seemed to puzzle all hands why I wanted to come to sea when I was doing so well at home and had so many clothes. I told them I came to sea to wear out my old clothes. We have not seen a sail for some time now. I have considerable anxiety to get to 'Frisco, now; and the first question with me will be "Who is President?" It seems to me now that could I be landed in 'Frisco safe, and hear from home just once, I would then be willing to die. at the same time I think I am better contented aboard this craft now than yet before; but I want the privilege of getting my feet once more on land and saying to myself, "I am myself?" For going to sea comes too much like under a tyrant's rule for me, brought up under the shadow of the Bunker-Hill Monument. I will give you an instance. The other day the mate and the second and third mates were taking the run, just after dinner. They thought the captain had gone below, but he came forward to see me—and the captain caught them nicely. When they saw him they were awfully frightened, and the mate threw down his quadrant and flew into his room. The second mate ran forward, and the third mate ran into the cabin. That was enough for me. It was something that wasn't taught me in Charlestown, to be afraid of an old gray-headed man. Last Sunday night the mate caught a large porpoise, and we had plenty of it to eat before it went overboard, one night, rather suddenly. But I am afraid if I keep on in this way my readers will take me for a regular growl about this ship.

December 30th, 1860. Sunday.

The "Dashing Wave" is on the line, they say she will not stay. Three more long tacks and she will make my buoys and bring old 'Frisco Bay. Today, we are in latitude 30°40'N—and near the longitude of 129 degrees west. During this month, we have had continual rainy and foggy weather and changing of winds, but rather light, which keeps the men continually hauling at the braces. When the men are at that work then is the time when you will hear growling, cursing, and braying, for the men are getting tired of the ship and of one another, while at the same time the carpenter is not very backward in telling how much he is in love with the captain and the mate. There is plenty of business going on at present in getting the ship ready to go into port. The men are over the side scrubbing paint and cleaning her off. This you may know they like, the ship going eight or ten knots with a good sea running, which gives them a good shower bath all the time. This would be bad enough if the weather were warm, but as it is I have to wear my woolen frock.

I have been at work all week on top of the after house. If the captain sees a place that looks black, he has it taken out and a graving piece put in so that now the top of the house is completely cut into atoms. He is so anxious for me to keep to work that most of the time that I have been at work there I have had to wear oil clothes and get completely wet through.

From that you may judge how agreeable it is to be carpenter of a ship with a Marblehead skin-flint for a captain and a Salem back-biter for a mate. I generally had forty or fifty minutes for dinner, but now the captain has cut it down to thirty minutes because the days are shorter and I cannot see to work before half past six in the morning and leave off a little after five. But then after I leave off work I have got all my tools to oil and clean before I go to bed; for should I leave them over night they would be nearly spoiled. I have made four large fenders out of an old cross-jack yard. All the time that I was at work on them the rain was coming down in torrents, but it was no use, I had to make them. I did plenty of blowing, you bet.

I will never go to work at noon unless the captain or mate comes after me, for I know that aboard of a ship the carpenter is entitled to one hour for dinner. The other day the captain sang out for me three times before I had got my dinner eaten, but I did not go, so he came forward and stood outside our house. I happened to look out and there he stood beckoning with his hand for me to come out. When I got ready, I went out and commenced work. They don't give me much cheek now, for I have too many friends aboard this ship, and another thing, she is getting too near 'Frisco. I should not be surprised to see a regular bloody knock-down and drag-out before we get in, or as soon as she gets into the wharf. Besides myself at work carpentering, there are employed from one to two men at work with the ship's tools, and often I have to lend them some of mine or else do the work myself. The mate thinks he is [something] at carpentering. Yesterday, the fore-tack bolt drew out again, and there is no place around the bow that is not entirely rotten.

The captain told me the other day that it was no use for me to try to come any of my dodges over him. I had to laugh in the man's face. He is so afraid he will get cheated that he thinks everybody is trying to cheat him. He is awfully down on the second mate who is as nice a man as ever I wish to see. The captain says the sailmaker is a bugger and the carpenter a hard nut, for with all his driving and blowing, I continue to gain flesh and have not had even a pimple on me while all hands, fore and aft, have been covered with sores and boils.

Christmas day the weather was quite inviting, but we had to work all day, and had our usual fare. Not the least respect was shown the day by the captain, although he pretends to belong to the church. When I turned out in the morning I wished all the folks at home a Merry Christmas, and often thought of home during the day. For supper I ate the last piece of the cake that sister Fannie gave me. I am in pretty good spirits now, all the time considering we are near 'Frisco. We have a fair wind now, and should it last we shall be in on Wednesday or Thursday; and whoever is on the wharf will have to stand out of the way when my chest comes over the side. Ever since the captain spoke to me about dodges, it has been the whole-go all over the ship, among the officers and men. "Look out for the Carpenter, he is up to dodges." Which, by the way, makes considerable sport. The second mate often sings it out to me, no matter whether the captain is near or not. The second mate said to me, on the poop, "I wish you and I had got into a better packet than this." He is pretty well acquainted in Charlestown; and one night he was up in "Evening Star" hall, and when he came down he stood looking into our hall door and Dan Ames invited him in. The way I knew it was that he picked Dan out among the daguerreotypes. The third mate is in my room all the spare time he can get. The second mate told him jokingly that he had better move his bed in there. He and I are pretty good chums, he loves the captain and the mate quite as well as I do. He is somewhat acquainted in Charlestown.

Last night, the captain sent a mince pie into our room, by the steward; but I told him he would have to pelt me with pies to come the soft solder over me. Thus far I have lived on salt grub and I can stand it the rest of the way. When I started from Boston, I thought that I could not get my money, except what I got in advance; but now I know I can get every cent; and when I get it into my hands I will tell him how dearly I love him and what a nice man he is, how well he uses his officers, how cool he is in a gale, how pleasant in a calm. But as it is getting dark, I must here close after first giving you our bill of fare,[4] for perhaps next Sunday I shall be in a place where time will be too precious to be used in writing journals.

---

4   See appendix B.

I arrived in 'Frisco on Saturday, after a passage of 143 days from Boston. We had a severe gale after making the light, and were blown out to sea and came near losing the ship on the rocks.

Very respectfully,
Your obedient servant,
Signed—Philip Hichborn, Jr.
Carpenter, Ship "Dashing Wave"

An 1889 photograph of clipper ship *Dashing Wave* tied up to the docks in San Francisco. (Photograph courtesy of the J. Porter Shaw Library, San Francisco Maritime National Historical Park.)

Appendix A.
Dashing Wave Sail Chart

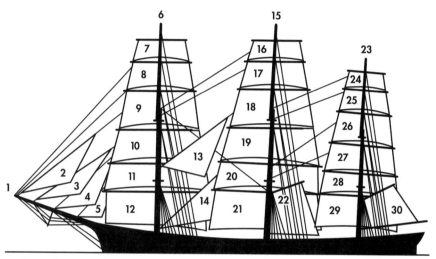

Chart showing sail arrangement of *Dashing Wave*. (Drawing by Mary H. Thiesen.)

No authentic sail plan for *Dashing Wave* is known to exist. The sail plan shown is typical of three-masted ships of the period and reflects the masting and sparring shown in photographs of *Dashing Wave*. *Dashing Wave* carried studding sails, but they cannot be shown in a profile view. For her appearance with studding sails set, see the drawing of *Dashing Wave* on the original manuscript cover.

1. Jib boom
2. Flying jib
3. Outer jib
4. Inner jib
5. Fore topmast staysail
6. Fore mast
7. Fore skysail

8. Fore royal
9. Fore topgallant
10. Fore upper topsail
11. Fore lower topsail
12. Foresail
13. Main topgallant staysail
14. Main topmast staysail

15. Main mast
16. Main skysail
17. Main royal
18. Main topgallant
19. Main upper topsail
20. Main lower topsail
21. Mainsail
22. Main spanker (or spencer)

23. Mizzen mast
24. Mizzen skysail
25. Mizzen royal
26. Mizzen topgallant
27. Mizzen upper topsail
28. Mizzen lower topsail
29. Crossjack (or mizzen)
30. Spanker

Appendix B.
Dashing Wave Bill of Fare

~~~~~~~~~~~~~~~~~~~~~~~~~~~~~~~~~~~~~~~

Philip Hichborn provided this bill of fare and "Remarks" at the end of the original manuscript. See Glossary of Nautical and Slang Terms for definitions of food items.

Monday:
morning: coffee and cracker hash
noon: water and dandy-funk
night: tea and salt beef

Tuesday:
morning: coffee and cracker hash
noon: water and baked beans
night: tea and salt pork

Wednesday:
morning: coffee and cracker hash
noon: rice and molasses
night: tea and salt beef

Thursday:
morning: coffee and cracker hash
noon: water, beef, and duff
night: tea and beef

Friday:
morning: coffee and cracker hash
noon: beef and baked rice
night: beef and tea

Saturday [omitted in journal, likely the following]:
morning: coffee and cracker hash
noon: water and some kind of meat
night: tea and beef

Sunday:
morning: coffee and cracker hash
noon: water, beef, and duff
night: tea and beef

Remarks: Occasionally we will have what is called a "tropical soup": the old soup cans that the preserved meats come in are boiled over in three or four buckets of water, this is set on for dessert; and sometimes of a morning, instead of cracker hash we will have mush and molasses, &c., &c.

Appendix C.
Remarks, about Ship *Dashing Wave*

Lyman H. Ellingwood, Passenger

I left Boston in this ship April 4th. She is an A1 clipper ship about 5 years old, 1200 tons register, commanded this voyage by the following officers and complement of men: D. R. Le Craw [*sic*], captain; Thomas Mayo Carter, 1st mate; William Perkins Shaw of Plimouth, 2nd mate; W. Webber Hughes of Boston, 3rd mate; sailmaker, carpenter, cook, steward, cabin boy, and 24 men before the mast and two boys.

The Captain is an old fogy, disagreeable to everyone. The 1st officer is a decent sort of a man. Mr. Shaw is a gentleman and a very smart young man, only 25 years old. Mr. Hughes goes by the name of Walking Dictionary. He is a fine young man, and quite smart.

The ship *Dashing Wave* is a smart sailer, goes 14 knots easily, enough to make the quickest of passages. Life at sea is divided into watches of 4 hours each, with the exception of the watches from 4 to 8 PM. These are called the Dog Watches, two hours each. Time at sea is kept by striking a given number of bells for each hour and half hour, thus the Watch being set at 12 o'clock noon, half-past 12 is one bell, 1 PM 2 bells, half-past 1 three bells, and so to 4 PM which is 8 bells. Then the Watch is changed, each watch being composed of 8 bells. The men are divided half and half into the watches. The starboard, or captain's watch, is commanded by the 2nd mate, and the port watch is commanded by the chief mate, who has the 3rd mate under him as one of his watch.

The sailors live on salt beef, pork, and hard bread. They are not always an awful set. Seldom you find an American in the forecastle of a ship, nothing but foreigners, by far the greater proportion do not know how to read or write. The carpenter or "chips" as the sea phrase is, and the sailmaker or "sails" (sailor term) live in the aft house as it is called, a small room in the after part of the house on deck forward, separate from the sailors. They consider themselves above the sailors. In most American ships, they eat their meals in the cabin at the 2nd table, but in this ship they are not allowed the privilege.

The captain has his wife with him. She is, or has been, a fine lady, but he has spoilt her by his meanness. Also Mr. Thomas Abbott is a passenger, he and I have a stateroom together.

Source: Logbook of ship *Dashing Wave*, 1859–1860 (145–46), M656, Log 1859D, Phillips Library, Peabody Essex Museum, Salem, Massachusetts.

Appendix D.
Philip Hichborn's Life after 1860

Hichborn's later life and career attest to his technical expertise, professionalism, and leadership ability. Not long after his arrival in San Francisco, he renewed his association with his mentor, naval constructor Melvin Simmons, and began working at the Mare Island Naval Shipyard. Hichborn advanced rapidly through civilian positions in the shipbuilding department at Mare Island. These jobs included journeyman shipwright, timber inspector, draftsman, and quarterman shipwright. By 1862, at the age of twenty-three, the navy promoted Hichborn to the senior position of master shipwright.[1] It is entirely possible that Hichborn learned many of the lessons of good management during the time he served on board *Dashing Wave*. In a brief piece documenting Hichborn's life, written late in his career, the unnamed writer notes that Hichborn earned an "enviable and merited reputation for excellent management and executive ability."[2]

After the Civil War, Hichborn began a successful career in the United States Navy. In 1869 Hichborn received an appointment as an assistant naval constructor, with a service rank equivalent to that of a lieutenant. Within a year, the navy ordered him to a new post, and the farewell ball in his honor attests to Hichborn's popularity with individuals of all ranks at Mare Island. From California Hichborn transferred to the Portsmouth Naval Shipyard in Kittery, Maine, where he served as assistant to the famous clipper ship designer and naval constructor, Samuel M. Pook. In 1875 the navy promoted Hichborn to full naval constructor with the relative rank of captain and transferred him to the Philadelphia Navy Yard. During his tenure there, Hichborn oversaw much of the work involved

---

1   Hamersly, 390.
2   "Philip Hichborn ... U.S.N.," 328.

Philip Hichborn in 1869 after receiving a commission in the U.S. Navy as an assistant naval constructor. Prior to receiving this commission, he had established himself as a highly competent master shipwright at the Mare Island Navy Yard near San Francisco. (Photograph courtesy of the Naval History and Heritage Command, Washington Navy Yard, Washington, D.C.)

Philip Hichborn (second from the right) as a member of the 1888 Naval Review Board. (Photograph courtesy of the Naval History and Heritage Command, Washington Navy Yard, Washington, D.C.)

in transferring shipyard operations from the old navy yard, near downtown Philadelphia, to a newer industrialized naval facility at League Island near the confluence of the Delaware River and Schuylkill River. The year he transferred to Philadelphia he married Jennie M. Franklin, and together they would raise a son and a daughter.[3]

By 1880 Hichborn began serving in influential positions relating to new naval construction. For example, he was selected by Navy Secretary William Hunt to serve on the first Naval Advisory Board, which initiated the process of modernizing the fleet from old wooden warships to modern steel vessels. From 1883 to 1889 he served as a member of the Board of Inspection and Survey, receiving orders to tour European navy yards and dockyards and compiling a report on modern European naval

3   Garraty and Carnes, eds., "Hichborn, Philip," vol. 10, 735; Malone, ed., 3.

Philip Hichborn later in life, in civilian attire, probably around the time of his 1901 retirement from the U.S. Navy. ("Philip Hichborn, Chief Naval Constructor, U.S.N." *Blue and Gray: The Patriotic American Magazine* 2 [July–December, 1893]: 326.)

shipbuilding facilities.[4] Congress published a first and second edition of his report, which became the standard text on late nineteenth-century naval shipbuilding technology. In 1884 the navy also appointed Hichborn chief naval constructor for the Washington Navy Yard, and he assumed the duties of assistant to the head of the navy's Bureau of Construction and Repair.[5]

The 1890s saw the culmination of Hichborn's lengthy career with the U.S. Navy. During this decade, he remained active in overseeing the technological transition of the navy's fleet from wooden sailing vessels to the steel steam-powered warships that comprised America's so-called

4   Hichborn, *European Dock-Yards.*
5   Skerrett, "Philip Hichborn," *Who's Who,* 899.

New Navy. At the same time he developed devices and appliances that improved the safety and effectiveness of naval service. These inventions included lifeboat designs, various shipfitting innovations, and gun turret improvements. By 1893 the navy appointed Hichborn the service's chief constructor, and he took control of the Bureau of Construction and Repair, receiving the rank of commodore. Hichborn's four-year term expired in 1897; however, the Navy Department saw fit to reappoint him for a second four-year term. In 1898 Hichborn faced the final challenge of his career and succeeded in preparing the navy's battle fleet for rapid deployment to fight the Spanish-American War, a conflict whose success relied heavily on the U.S. Navy.[6]

In 1901, after a long and productive career, Philip Hichborn retired as a rear admiral, but he remained active in professional matters. In retirement he served as an advisor in naval shipbuilding matters and as a writer and a member of professional societies. As the journal "Cruise of the *Dashing Wave*" attests, Hichborn always remained faithful to his family and friends and his hometown of Charlestown. In his journal's text, Hichborn regularly recalls memories of boyhood friends, family members, and favorite places in Charlestown. Before retiring he compiled a genealogical history of his family, dating back to 1673.[7]

On May 1, 1910, Philip Hichborn died in Washington, D.C., after a long illness. His remains were returned to Boston to be interred in a cemetery near his old home in Charlestown.[8]

---

6 Hamersly, 390; "Admiral Hichborn Dead," *New York Times*, May 2, 1910, 9; Malone, ed., 3.

7 Malone, ed., 3; Hichborn, "Chronology."

8 "Admiral Hichborn Dead," *New York Times*, May 2, 1910, 9.

Appendix E.
Clipper Ship *Dashing Wave* after 1860

After Hichborn's 1860 passage, *Dashing Wave* had a very long and eventful career. The clipper sailed primarily between domestic locations, but she also called at international ports such as Melbourne, Sydney, Manila, Calcutta, and Hong Kong.

During the Civil War a cannonball became embedded in *Dashing Wave*'s hull. It was rumored that the famous Confederate raider CSS *Alabama* put it there; however, a more reliable source indicates that the incident occurred when the clipper departed Galveston, Texas, with a load of cotton. In 1864 *Dashing Wave* sustained damage on a passage from Hong Kong, and in 1867 she grounded on shoals near New York Harbor and sank off Sandy Hook, New Jersey. By 1869 the clipper had been refloated and refurbished for a voyage to San Francisco. During that passage, gales around Cape Horn did considerable damage to the vessel's spars and rigging, and the ship's captain died.[1]

During the 1870s *Dashing Wave* joined numerous vessels transporting the building supplies that helped develop America's western frontier. The clipper was altered for hauling lumber and, working out of Tacoma, Washington Territory, carried wood and coal along the West Coast. In the 1880s and 1890s *Dashing Wave* also carried lumber to exotic locations such as Hawaii, the South Pacific, and Alaska's Klondike.

By the turn of the century the ascendancy of steam propulsion and the increasing difficulty of obtaining profitable cargoes made the overhaul and rerigging of tall ships uneconomical. In 1902 *Dashing Wave* was sold to new owners who cut down the masts and converted the once-proud tall ship into a utility barge.[2]

---

1 Brighton, 91; Fairburn, vol. 3, 1624, 1889. See appendix F for discussion of the embedded cannon ball.
2 See appendix F; also Brighton, 92–94.

Not only did *Dashing Wave* have an eventful career, she outlived all but a few of her wooden counterparts. Throughout much of the journal's narrative, Hichborn complains about the poor condition of *Dashing Wave*; however, the ship maintained a reputation for solid construction throughout much of her career. *Dashing Wave*'s hull remained sound throughout the nearly twenty years she served as a barge.

The clipper ship's career came to an end in March 1920. While under tow to an Alaskan salmon cannery with a full load of canning supplies, *Dashing Wave* grounded in Alaska's treacherous Seymour Narrows. So ended her lengthy and colorful career.[3]

---

3   Brighton, 95–96; Fairburn, vol. 4, 2334.

A 1912 close-up of the barge *Dashing Wave* in Puget Sound, Washington. Note the vessel's cut-down masts and bowsprit and the derricks attached to the main and mizzen masts. (Photograph courtesy of the J. Porter Shaw Library, San Francisco Maritime National Historical Park.)

A 1912 photograph of tug boat *Goliah*, of the Puget Sound Tug Boat Company, pulling the barge *Dashing Wave* in Puget Sound, Washington. (Photograph courtesy of the J. Porter Shaw Library, San Francisco Maritime National Historical Park.)

Appendix F.
Captain Lancaster's Daughter, Irene Johnson, Discusses *Dashing Wave*

The original transcript of this interview, conducted by Karl Kortum and Austin Keegan in October 1962, is held by the J. Porter Shaw Library of the San Francisco Maritime National Historic Park. Omissions of irrelevant discussion are indicated in square brackets.

Austin Keegan: We're going out to see Irene Johnson, the daughter of Captain Richard Lancaster.

Karl Kortum: Captain Lancaster was one of the most famous captains on the Pacific Coast, wasn't he?

Austin Keegan: He was, perhaps, one of the greatest. 1876 [*sic*], I believe, he was captain of the old *Dashing Wave*.

Karl Kortum: The *Dashing Wave* was a true clipper ship.

Austin Keegan: She was.

[Omission]

Austin Keegan: What's your earliest recollection of the *Dashing Wave?*

Irene Johnson: I can remember her because I was older.

Karl Kortum: You were in the *Canada* first and then the *Dashing Wave?*

Irene Johnson: Yes, we went to sea a lot on the *Dashing Wave.*

Karl Kortum: Did the *Dashing Wave* lay up at Antioch [California]?

Irene Johnson: No, she never laid up there. The *Dashing Wave* sailed most of the time. We loaded at Tacoma as a rule. It must have been better times. Lumber.

Karl Kortum: About what year did your father take her over?

Irene Johnson: I was about six.

Austin Keegan: 1897.

Irene Johnson: Yeah, in around there, 1897 or '98.

Karl Kortum: How long did your father have her?

Irene Johnson: Well he had her quite a few years. Up until we brought the first load of lumber to Alaska; Nome. We were children then. Of course we lay at anchor. There were no docks or anything. It was very hard to get ashore. You went ashore in a boat. You'd ride in on a wave and rest on the bottom, then you'd ride in on the next one and rest, until you got close enough to get out.

[Omission]

Karl Kortum: You then went to Seattle?

Irene Johnson: No, we went back to Puget Sound; Tacoma.

Karl Kortum: You had left from Tacoma?

Irene Johnson: With a load of lumber. That's what they wanted then. They wanted to build shelters for the winter. My mother couldn't sleep because the sun shone the whole time. They worked quite a bit at night. Then we came back and I think my father made another trip up there. That was the end of the *Dashing Wave*. You know after she was turned over . . .

[Omission]

Karl Kortum: Was that when she was made into a barge?

Irene Johnson: Yes, shortly thereafter.

Austin Keegan: He sailed her right into the dock and people could understand . . .

Irene Johnson: Yes, my father sailed with the *Dashing Wave* right up to the Long Wharf in Oakland, right up alongside. But you could handle her. When we went up to Alaska; when we went through Unimak Pass

up there. You know he lashed the rudder and backed his sail—foresail—
you know and she [backed] right astern like a steamer. Instead of tacking
that's the way he did it, going back and forth across the straits. You could
handle her just like a yacht. Oh he loved her. His heart and soul was
in her. When he left her it took years off him. If anybody even marred
the woodwork on her it was like they drove a knife in him. She had a
beautiful cabin. It was all white and it had an aqua blue—just a narrow
strip that went between the fancy moldings. Then the gilt. Oh she was
beautiful.

Karl Kortum: The cabin was finished out in white?

Irene Johnson: Yes, you know the ferryboats did that for a while. They
had their interiors painted and they had a trim of blue and gold. I think
that was the style in those days for the cabins. She had a beautiful cabin.
And her dining room—we had an oblong table and the seats were made
with a back that you could go back and put them up against the table with
your back to the table so you switch it this way to eat. And the mizzen
mast went right down through the table.

[Omission]

Karl Kortum: The *Dashing Wave* was sold to be a barge and it was no
wish of your father's, and he had to leave her?

Irene Johnson: He left her.

[Omission]

Karl Kortum: What comparison would you make between the *Dashing
Wave* and the *W. J. Patterson?*

Irene Johnson: They were different builds and the quarters were laid out
different too. The *Patterson* was very nice too. Very comfortable, a very
nice ship.

Karl Kortum: The *Dashing Wave* was, I imagine, far more elegant.

Irene Johnson: Well, the *Patterson*, her woodwork was all polished with
varnish. It was all wood. It was mahogany or something. The *Dashing
Wave* had the white cabin with the trim on it. And we had a beautiful

table on the *Dashing Wave*. It came from Manila. They cut a big slab and the bark was right around the edge and polished very highly on the top. It stood on the base with the bark on it and legs coming out to keep it steady.

Karl Kortum: This was in the dining . . .

Irene Johnson: No, in the cabin.

Karl Kortum: It was just an ornamental . . .

Irene Johnson: Yes, it was quite a large table.

Karl Kortum: Do you recall any other fixtures in the cabin?

Irene Johnson: Well, the white and the blue and the gold.

[Omission]

Irene Johnson: Oh, my father loved the *Dashing Wave*; he could do anything with it.

Karl Kortum: She was a real clipper.

Irene Johnson: But this one, the *Canada*, my father said he'd sail into the Bay; sail up to the wharf and the people would run. He said she was miserable. It took two men at the wheel if it was bad weather.

Karl Kortum: She was very full lines, she's no aristocrat like the *Dashing Wave*.

Austin Keegan: The *Dashing Wave* was a thoroughbred, this one here . . .

Karl Kortum: We have a fine photograph, a big one, down at the museum of the *Dashing Wave* in her final days as a barge. She lasted until 1922 or so.

Karl Kortum: You say your father found a cannon ball in the *Dashing Wave*?

Irene Johnson: Yes, in the *Dashing Wave* when she was running during the Civil War.

An 1898 photograph of visitors at the bow of *Dashing Wave* in Port Los Angeles, California. Note what appear to be two furled jibs and a furled fore topmast staysail. (Photograph courtesy of the J. Porter Shaw Library, San Francisco Maritime National Historical Park.)

Karl Kortum: Blockade running?

Irene Johnson: Yes. It just rested right in the rib. It didn't go through. It just lay right in the rib and when they were doing some repair work they came on it. Of course my father took it out and gave it to the museum over in the park. Loaned it.

Karl Kortum: I'm interested in your account of—I assume it was the mate's desire—to paint the *Dashing Wave* in a way that would conceal

An 1898 photograph of clipper ship *Dashing Wave* moored along the docks at Port Los Angeles, California. (Photograph courtesy of the J. Porter Shaw Library, San Francisco Maritime National Historical Park.)

the fact that she was "hogged" as the expression goes. Could you comment on that?

Irene Johnson: Oh, you mean when the artist was painting her, he wanted to make her look like she did when she was first launched and my father wanted her painted just like she was.

Karl Kortum: Oh, you meant the oil painting of the ship. That's the painting we have; the museum.

Irene Johnson: Yes, he wouldn't have it.

Karl Kortum: You say that she was the apple of his eye?

Irene Johnson: Yes, she was. He kept her well too, just like a yacht.

Karl Kortum: I think she was built in 1953 [*sic*] as I remember. Yes, the *Dashing Wave* was a famous ship on the West Coast.

[Omission]

Austin Keegan: She was finally burned, wasn't she?

Karl Kortum: No, she was towing as a barge up in . . .

Irene Johnson: No they sold her. Father had her the last trip and it broke his heart to leave. Up in Alaska. They used her for towing, as a barge.

Karl Kortum: She towed for at least twenty years.

Irene Johnson: Was she lost?

Karl Kortum: As I remember, a line parted in a gale and she went ashore.

Irene Johnson: Yes, she went ashore and broke up.

Karl Kortum: I imagine she was still pretty fast.

Irene Johnson: Oh, she always was. She was the apple of his eye. He could handle her. I've seen him take and lash the rudder and turn the yards and back her up just like a steamer.

Karl Kortum: That was tacking through Unimak pass?

Irene Johnson: Yes.

Karl Kortum: In other words, back across and haul the yards around . . .

Irene Johnson: Sometimes, when we were going on a long trip, she would go for weeks without anybody at the wheel.

Austin Keegan: Just with the balance of the sail.

Irene Johnson: Just put the rudder over and let her go. She was beautiful. My father's love for her, we felt the same way.

Karl Kortum: The quarters that the family occupied aboard, you called that the cabin?

Irene Johnson: Yes.

Karl Kortum: That was right aft. That was the big room, then the little rooms opened off of that?

Irene Johnson: Yes. She had a beautiful cabin. It ran right across. You see there was an alleyway that went right around the cabins. In the *Dashing Wave* there was a passageway all around and then there were windows into the cabin.

Karl Kortum: On deck?

Irene Johnson: Yes.

Karl Kortum: Then you had those sliding windows on the *Dashing Wave*? Windows with the wooden flag on them I suppose.

Irene Johnson: I've forgotten exactly. They opened onto the deck around the rail so you could walk around them.

Karl Kortum: You called the room forward of the cabin the dining room. You didn't use the term "saloon"?

Irene Johnson: No, we called it the dining room. Maybe the men . . . no, I never heard . . .

Karl Kortum: Maybe a British word. The mates would eat with you?

Irene Johnson: There were two tables and the mates ate with my father. The others ate at the next setting.

Karl Kortum: The mate ate with the family and after you left the second mate . . .

Irene Johnson: And the carpenter usually ate aft too. The donkey man; he was a carpenter.

Austin Keegan: The bosun?

Irene Johnson: No, they called him carpenter.

Karl Kortum: Had he been with your father a long time?

Irene Johnson: Yes, my father held his crew a long time.

Karl Kortum: Do you remember his name?

Irene Johnson: No.

Karl Kortum: Did you have a steward as well as a cook?

Irene Johnson: No, they had a cook and a cabin boy.

Karl Kortum: British had a steward and a cook but you didn't have a steward that lived aft? And the cook didn't live aft?

Irene Johnson: No, I think he had a room off the galley.

Karl Kortum: And the ship had a donkey engine? You don't remember anything about the donkey engine? Any incidents. It didn't blow up or anything?

Irene Johnson: Oh no. I remember one time they used to have certain things on certain days, what they call plum duff. We used to be crazy about it. They had it once or twice a week, I think on Sunday. It was a real treat. Anyway, you know how kids are. We were running around past the galley and I catch a glimpse of plum duff. It was all mixed. There was a little seat that the cabin boy sat on when he peeled the potatoes. Under the seat there was this mixture, boy that cured me. The next time he comes aft with the plum duff, and he brings it in and cuts it, I didn't want any. Elvina looks at me and says, "What's the matter?" "Nothing," I said. "Well, then I don't want any either." So he says to my mother, "Mrs., what's the matter with the children, they used to be so fond of plum duff? They won't take it any more."

Karl Kortum: Did you tell him?

Irene Johnson: No. That cured me. I never ate plum duff again.

Karl Kortum: Did you have a Japanese cook?

Irene Johnson: No, he was a white man. We had Japanese cooks though. I think he must have made a batch that lasted a month.

Karl Kortum: How did you bathe?

Irene Johnson: On the *Dashing Wave*, if I remember right they didn't have a big bathroom. My mother used to bathe us in a tub. Any time it was raining my mother was always collecting water. Every bucket, anything that would hold water.

Karl Kortum: What was done about laundry?

Irene Johnson: One time there was plenty of water so my mother washed the clothes and then she said, "Well, I have to have a line to hang them up." My father says, "I can't be bothered with lines across the deck." My mother says, "How am I going to dry them?" so he inveigles my mother into putting the clothes on the line and he hoists it up on the halyard up to the top of the mast. Of course children, you know, used to wear nice white or light clothes. Well, they get them up there and the breeze comes along and starts to whip them up in the ratlines with that tar stuff. Of course when my mother took them down, they were worse than before. My mother was furious. I always wondered what would happen if we ever came on a ship; they would wonder what kind of signals we were flying.

Karl Kortum: It must have been quite a problem on a ship. Fresh water for washing.

Irene Johnson: One time when we were up in Puget Sound on the *Dashing Wave*, the ship needed cleaning on the bottom and it was a big expense to go in the dry dock so they just keeled her over on the beach. We went ashore and camped on the beach and they put a rope to the mast and a tree and pulled her right over and cleaned her on one side and the next day when the tide came and she floated up, the next day they turned her around. It took two or three or maybe four days. [See "careening" in Glossary of Nautical and Slang Terms.] We also went ashore there one time when he wanted to fumigate it. They were getting bed bugs in the fo'c'sle. We used to have books and magazines and when we were finished with them we'd pass them back to the men. But he never allowed any to come back. He didn't want bed bugs or cockroaches from the galley aft. We were so careful. We went ashore and he closed everything and he fumigated. Everybody went ashore.

Karl Kortum: That must have been a lark.

Irene Johnson: Oh it was; especially for the children. We were off the ship and we could run along the beach.

Karl Kortum: That must have been quite a thing to see, the ship rolled over. In the heaving down process, I imagine he used the ship's own crew.

Irene Johnson: All by hand.

Karl Kortum: The cook went ashore to cook for all the men?

Irene Johnson: Sure.

Karl Kortum: That was a real exercise in seamanship. How effective was the fumigation?

Irene Johnson: When we came back, oh for two or three days you could smell the sulphur.

Karl Kortum: Well, it's been a real pleasure to talk to someone who was raised on a clipper ship.

Glossary of Nautical and Slang Terms

aback, taken: The situation when the wind bears against the front surfaces of the sails caused by a sudden wind shift or the helmsman's inattention. In heavy weather, this is quite dangerous and could cause dismasting.

adze: A wood-cutting tool shaped like a short-handled garden hoe, with the blade set at a right angle to the handle.

aloft, going: Climbing up into the rigging. On *Dashing Wave*, seamen typically would go aloft by climbing the standing rigging on the weather side, using ratlines secured crossways to the shrouds.

back biter: Someone who says mean or spiteful things about another.

backing sail: Backfilling a sail to aid in maneuvering a sailing vessel.

backstay: A rope or cable support for a mast, running from the masthead aft to the deck or to another mast.

bark: A ship, typically three-masted, that is square-rigged on the fore and main masts and fore-and-aft rigged on the mizzen. Also spelled "barque."

batten: A thin strip of wood used to seal and reinforce a joint or to secure a hatch tarpaulin to the deck. Also strips of wood inserted in pockets in a sail to help it maintain its shape.

bean day: Crew's term for a day with little food and a head wind.

bear: A surly person.

belaying pin: A removable iron or wooden pin that fits into the pin rail or fife rail, to which rigging lines are attached.

bell, ship's: Bell used on board ships to strike the time and used in heavy fog to warn other vessels.

berth, sleeping: A place to sleep on board a ship; often a bunk.

bilge: The lowest part of ship's interior hull, where water and waste collect.

blackball: To ostracize or exclude socially.

Black Ball packet: A packet ship of the Black Ball Line, a successful nineteenth-century transatlantic shipping firm.

bleeding: To let out a person's blood; used as a treatment for disease prior to the introduction of modern medical practices.

block: A pulley or set of pulleys encased in a metal or wooden shell, used for hoisting or other purposes, such as bracing yards. Blocks were made in many configurations, some movable and others, such as cheek blocks, permanently attached.

blows/blower: A braggart; one who brags or boasts. A "New York" blower probably is a big city braggart.

boil: A sore or localized inflammation caused by infection.

bonnet: An additional piece of canvas laced to the foot of a jib or fore-and-aft sail to gather more wind. Also used to secure the foot of an upper-topsail to a lower-topsail yard.

booby hatch: A sliding hatch or cover.

boom: A spar used to extend the bottom of a fore-and-aft sail or to extend the yards to carry studding sails.

bowsprit: Large spar protruding from the bow of a ship used to support headsails.

boy: The rank of an inexperienced seaman.

brace: A rope used to swing a ship's yard horizontally.

braying: Making a harsh noise, similar to the sound of a donkey call.

brick, a perfect: A good-hearted person.

brig: A two-masted, square-rigged ship.

bugger: A worthless person or rascal.

bulkheads: The vertical partitions that divide a ship's spaces into separate compartments.

bulwark(s): The solid side of a ship built above the upper deck.

buntlines: A rope attached to the foot of a square sail to haul it up to the yard for furling.

butt: The end of a plank, board, or piece of lumber. Also a cask used to store liquids.

cable: A rope or chain used as the anchor line.

cable length: A maritime unit of length, reckoned as one tenth of a nautical mile, or 100 fathoms. Definitions vary.

capstan: A vertical, spindle-mounted drum used to lift heavy weights, such as the anchor. On nineteenth-century sailing ships the assembly was manually rotated using long wooden capstan bars (typically eight) and the capstan was "walked around." See also **windlass.**

careening: Heeling a ship down on one side by moving ballast, and/ or applying a strong purchase to her mast from an anchor point on shore, for the purpose of cleaning or repairing her underwater hull.

caulking: Material, such as oakum, driven into seams between planks to make them watertight.

chain hook: A chain with a hook shackled to the end.

cheek block: In *Dashing Wave* usage, a block permanently attached to a surface, typically a yardarm, through which a sheet is rove.

chest: A small trunk for storing one's clothes.

chock: A wedge or block used for steadying items and holding them motionless.

clew: The lower corners of square sails and the after corner of fore-and-aft sails.

clewing: To draw the clews of a square sail to the yard, as for furling.

cock wouldn't crow/could not make the cock crow: Could not intimidate others.

come the double over me: To trick or deceive.

come the possum over me: To trick or deceive.

come the soft sodder [solder] over me: Probably to deceive by false expressions or gestures of friendship.

counter, stern: The part of the stern that extends behind and overhangs the waterline.

cracker hash: A combination of alternate layers of salt beef, peas, and ship's biscuit. Also called "sea pie." See also appendix B, *Dashing Wave* Bill of Fare.

cross-jack (or crojack): The lower crossed yard on the mizzenmast.

cross-trees: Horizontal iron or wood spars located at the lower mastheads to support the top. Topmast cross-trees also support the topgallant mast backstay spreaders.

daguerreotype: An early nineteenth-century form of photograph produced on a silvered copper plate.

dandy funk: A pudding made of crumbled hardtack, fat, and molasses. Also known as "danderfunk." See also appendix B, *Dashing Wave* Bill of Fare.

diamonds: Diamond-shaped pieces of wood used to replace knots and small areas of damaged or rotten wood.

dips/dipping into him: Author's term for treating one poorly.

dodges/dodges over him: Tricks or deception.

dog: A wood or iron fitting set in the topgallant masthead that secures a sheave or fairlead and allows the chain "tye" to run freely when the topgallant yard is raised or lowered.

dog-house: Typically a short deckhouse or raised hatchway above the level of the cabin top. Hichborn's comment, made only twelve days after departing Boston, suggests that this was a dog-house built for the captain's dog.

dog vane: A small weather vane made of feathers, yarn, or light line to show the wind's direction.

dog watches: Half watches of two hours each, from 4:00 to 6:00 p.m. and from 6:00 to 8:00 p.m.

donkey/donkey engine: A small (usually steam) engine found in large sailing vessels for hoisting sails, working the windlass, or handling cargo. The man in charge of the donkey engine was called "the donkeyman."

downhaul: A rigging line used to pull the upper topsail and upper topgallant yards down to their lowest positions. Only upper topsail and upper topgallant yards have downhauls. Also, a line used to haul a sail down for furling.

duff/plum duff: A term used by seamen for a stiff flour-and-water pudding boiled in a bag and eaten with molasses. Plum duff also contained raisins or currants. The Royal Navy referred to duff as "hasty pudding," a term well known to all Harvard graduates.

Dutchman: American-born sailor's term for a sailor born in Europe.

earing: A rope used to fasten a sail corner to the yard.

equator ("the Line"): Midway point between the north and south poles (zero degrees latitude).

eye bolt: A bolt with a looped head for holding a hook or rope.

fender: A wood or rope object hung over the ship's side to protect it from chafing while moored alongside a dock or another vessel.

fife rail: A rail surrounding the mast, with holes for inserting belaying pins. See also **pin rail**.

fish: In carpentry, a fished joint typically is used to connect two boards or timbers that must be joined end to end or to repair a long timber or spar that has been broken or damaged. Fish pieces may be of wood or iron and usually are added to both sides of the joint to increase its strength.

flunky: One performing menial duties.

foot ropes: Ropes strung below the yards to support seamen while reefing or furling square sails.

forecastle: A compartment located forward of the foremast, housing the seamen's quarters.

fore hatch: The forward cargo hatch.

foremast: The mast nearest the bow of the ship.

furling sail: To roll or fold a sail and secure it.

futtock shrouds: A set of small shrouds that lead down from the mast top to the mast or lower shrouds where they are fastened.

gaff: Free swinging spar on which the top of a fore-and-aft sail is secured.

galley: The kitchen on board a ship.

***Gaspée*/*Gaspée 9* boy**: The reference to Bill Robinson's being a *Gaspée 9* boy, although obviously complimentary, is unclear. The *Gaspée* was a British revenue schooner sent to Rhode Island in 1772 to enforce customs collection and inspect cargo. She ran aground in Narragansett Bay on June 9, 1772, and was boarded and burned by a group of Rhode Island citizens. The incident occurred 88 years before Hichborn's voyage.

gone goose: A person for whom there is no hope or one in a hopeless situation.

gooseneck: An iron universal joint used to attach a lower yard to the mast in such a manner that it is free to move in any direction. The weight of the lower yard is supported by a chain sling, not by the gooseneck; the gooseneck secures the yard to the mast and allows it to be braced 'round.

graving (or **graven**) **piece:** A new piece of wood fashioned to replace the rotted area of a ship.

greeny (or **greenness**): A beginner or rookie or a person displaying the qualities thereof.

growl: Someone who behaves in an angry way.

growling, growly: Complaining angrily.

half breeder: Derisive term for another.

halyards (or **halliards**): Lines used to raise and lower sails and yards.

hard knocks: Hichborn uses this term in two contexts, referring to fights among the crew and the experience of bad weather and heavy seas.

hard nut: A person not easily intimidated.

hatch/hatchway: A square or rectangular opening in the ship's deck allowing access to cargo holds and areas below deck. Typically there are three main hatchways: fore, main, and after. During a voyage, hatchways are secured by hatch covers.

hatch house: Hichborn makes brief mention of a hatch house in his diary. Typically, it is a small, temporary deckhouse built over a ship's cargo hatch during a voyage and removed while the ship is in port. The building of hatch houses was common among the clipper ship fleet.

head: A shipboard toilet.

head reaching: A condition of sail trim intermediate between heaving to and beating to windward. That is, setting just enough sail, properly trimmed, to keep the vessel going ahead without forcing it and risking dismasting. When heaving to, a vessel is trying to make as little headway as possible; when head reaching, the vessel is trying to make as much headway, and as little leeway, as possible.

head sea: A sea coming head-on to the ship.

heave to: To stop a vessel's forward progress by holding the helm in opposition to the force of the sails.

hermaphrodite brig: A two-masted vessel with a square-rigged foremast and a fore-and-aft main. The term is obsolete, and the rig is now known as a brigantine.

hogged: A condition in which the ends of the vessel droop lower than the midship part. This stresses the keel and bottom members in compression, and the deck and top members in tension. The opposite condition is known as "sagging."

hold trumps: To have an advantage over another.

hoops, mast: Wooden rings encircling the mast that allow fore-and-aft sails to slide up and down a mast or standing rigging.

house (after, forward): A deckhouse located on board ship.

hull down: A ship seen at a distance so that, because of the curvature of the earth, only her masts and sails are seen.

jack-knife mate: An untrained assistant.

jack-stay: Rope stretched taut along the yard to which a square sail is attached.

jib: A triangular fore-and-aft headsail, normally fixed to the bowsprit ahead of the foremast.

keel: The lowest, and principal, timber of a ship, running fore and aft and supporting the frames. The keel, which provides longitudinal strength to the hull, generally is composed of several heavy timbers scarfed together. The stem and sternposts can be considered extensions of the keel.

knock down: 1. A fight; short for "knock-down-drag-out." 2. A vessel lying on her beam ends, from which she does not recover, is said to be "knocked down."

landlubber: A derisive term used by sailors to describe a person who is not a seaman (that is, one who lives on land).

large enough to eat hay: Author's term for livestock, such as cows.

latitude: The distance north or south of the equator, expressed in degrees.

Line, the: The equator.

longboat: The largest open boat on a merchant vessel used to transport men and materials between the ship and shore or to other ships.

longitude: The distance east or west of the prime meridian in Greenwich, England, and expressed in degrees.

luff: A term usually used for the forward edge of a fore-and-aft sail. Hichborn uses it to refer to the fullest or roundest part of *Dashing Wave*'s bows.

make sail: To unfurl and set sails.

masthead: The top of the mast.

mast top: A platform, placed at the head of a lower mast, to spread the rigging and for the convenience of men working aloft.

mate: A ship's officer. The first mate ranks just below the captain and serves as the executive officer. The second and third mates rank in descending order.

mean: Stingy, cheap, or penurious.

molding: A decorative or recessed surface providing ornamentation.

mutiny: Revolt or resistance against a superior or an officer.

nasty: Personally filthy or unclean; physically repugnant.

nigger: Typically a vulgar term used for an African American; may not have been considered derisive by 1860 cultural norms.

oakum: Commonly a twisted hemp or jute fiber impregnated with pine tar or a tarlike substance. White oakum is made from untarred materials.

officers: The captain and first, second, and third mates.

oil clothes: Clothes treated with oil for greater water resistance.

old head: Context suggests that Hichborn means a youth wise beyond his years.

one row of teeth, acts as if he has: To behave like an ordinary person.

parcelling: A narrow strip of tarred canvas wound around a rope prior to serving.

parrel: A sliding metal hoop or band used to secure a hoisting yard to the mast and allowing it to be raised or lowered.

pay a seam: Sealing a seam by driving in tarred oakum with a caulking iron and mallet and then coating the seam with pitch (preferably hot). The expression, "The devil to pay and no pitch hot," derives from this practice. The devil was a curved deck seam that was difficult to pay and also the long seam between the keel and the adjoining hull planking. Paying an outboard seam while hanging from a harness places the unfortunate seaman "between the devil and the deep blue sea." See also **pitch** and **tar**.

pay off (the crew): To pay the crew wages at the end of the voyage.

pay off (the ship): When a ship's bow or head falls off from the direction of the wind.

pimp: Author's derogatory remark.

pin rail: Rack of belaying pins set on the ship's sides abreast of the masts and used for securing running rigging. See also **fife rail.**

pitch (noun): The words "pitch" and "tar" are used ambiguously. *Dashing Wave* probably used a pine tar–derived pitch, but the details are lacking. An 1886 USDA bulletin describes naval pitch as "pine tar that has been boiled down to 2/3 of its weight, to which rosin is added." It is used hot for sealing the caulked seams of a wooden vessel. See also **pay a seam** and **tar.**

pitch (verb): The movement of a ship about its transverse axis.

plane: To smooth or shape a wooden surface using a hand plane.

plank: A thick board used for planking the ship's hull, for decking, and for other purposes.

plank sheer: The course of planking covering the timber heads of the ship's frames.

plum duff: See **duff/plum duff.**

point to windward, getting a: Allowing someone an advantage.

poop deck: Technically called a "stern deck," it is a raised, partial deck located over the ship's after deck. It usually constitutes the roof of an after cabin, also known as the "poop cabin."

pooped, to be: To take a following sea or breaking wave over the stern of a ship. As it is extremely dangerous, ships that habitually were pooped were known as "wet ships."

port side: The left side of the ship.

poultice: Soft heated mass applied to skin sores and boils.

quadrant: A reflecting instrument used to measure the altitude above the horizon of the sun, moon, and stars and thereby determine the ship's position. Latitude was readily determined by these sightings; longitude was more difficult, requiring an accurate ship's chronometer.

queer: Differing in some odd way from the usual.

ratlines: Small ropes running horizontally across the shrouds, used by seamen going aloft.

reefing: Reducing the area of a sail by furling or tying it to its yard or boom.

reef points: A short tie or strap used to secure the reefed portion of the sail.

reef tackle: A tackle used to haul the middle of a sail up to the yard to ease the sail-reefing process.

reeve: To pass the end of a rope through a hole, block, or any aperture.

rigging (running): Rigging that is used to operate the sails or gear of a vessel or that runs through blocks.

rigging (standing): Fixed rigging that supports the masts and the spars. It is not moved when operating the vessel.

rolling: The motion of a ship about its longitudinal axis. A "stiff" ship has a short, jerky roll that will strain the standing rigging and is dangerous for the men working aloft. A "tender" ship has an easy roll, but is less stable under sail and requires greater skill in handling in stormy weather. She will put her lee rail under and ship green water over her deck. Hichborn says *Dashing Wave* "is a pretty bad roller, but she rolls long and low so it isn't so trying" (that is, she's a tender vessel).

row: A quarrel; to have a quarrel.

rudder screw gear: Gear allowing the ship's wheel to turn the rudder.

sailmaker: Crewman responsible for making and mending sails.

sailor's shirt: Wearing a damp shirt to dry it.

sails: See appendix A, *Dashing Wave* Sail Chart.

salt-horse, salt junk: A seaman's term for salt beef.

saucy: Bold and impudent.

scarph: A strong joint for overlapping timbers, formed by notching the pieces that fit together. A vessel's keel typically is formed from scarphed timbers, as were built-up wooden masts.

scuppers: Holes cut through the ship's sides to drain water off the deck. See also **side ports, waterways.**

scurvy: A disease of vitamin deficiency marked by soft gums, loose teeth, ulcerations, and bleeding into the skin and mucous membranes. Untreated scurvy invariably is fatal.

sea pie: A combination of alternate layers of salt beef, peas, and ship's biscuit. Also called "cracker hash." See also appendix B, *Dashing Wave* Bill of Fare.

serve: To wind fine line or spun yarn around a rope to prevent chafing.

shackle: A link in a chain cable fitted with a removable bolt, so the chain can be separated.

sheet: A rope used in setting or controlling a sail. With boom sails and staysails, sheets move the sails horizontally.

shorten sail: To reduce sail.

shrouds: The standing rigging that provides lateral bracing for main, top, and topgallant masts. Shrouds are set up very taut, using deadeyes and lanyards, or rigging screws. See also **ratlines.**

side ports: Openings cut in the side of the bulwarks to allow water trapped on the deck to drain overboard. See also **scuppers.**

skinflint: A miser. Used to describe the captain.

skysail: A high sail, set above the royals. Some ships also carried moonsails, which were set above the skysails. The benefit of using these small sails was minimal, and, as crews became smaller, most merchant ships did not set them.

slings: The chains used to support the center of a lower yard. The lower yard is not raised or lowered, and it typically is secured to the mast by a flexible gooseneck and two truss bands.

smiling as a basket of chips: To wear a big smile.

sou'wester: A waterproof hat with a wide slanting brim longer in back than in front.

spanker: The fore-and-aft gaffsail on the after mast of a ship or bark. Also called a "driver."

spar: A general term for a yard, boom, gaff, or other long wooden structural member, typically one that carries a sail.

spike: A large, hammer-driven nail or metal fastener.

squall: A sudden violent wind often accompanied by rain or snow.

staff (dog-vane): A stick used to support the dog vane.

staging: Planks or boards arranged into a platform, usually outboard.

start the music: Begin a fight or angry confrontation.

stern: The aft end of a ship.

sternway: Movement of a ship backward.

steward: A crew member responsible for serving food to the rest of the crew.

stove (noun): Typically a coal-burning device used for cooking and heat.

stove (verb): Broken in. When damage is done to the upper part of the hull, she is said to be "stove"; when damaged below the waterline, she is said to be "bilged." Damage (and usage) often was not that precise (for example, the whaleship *Essex* was "stove by a whale").

stowaway: An individual that hides on board a ship to obtain transportation.

studding sail: A light sail carried outside a square sail to increase the sail area. They are attached to studding sail yards, which are carried by studding sail booms.

swell: A long, large crestless wave.

tack: A rope used to haul the lower outer clew of the studding sail to the end of the boom.

tacked ship: A ship that has been turned to change course. Used by Hichborn to describe a change of mind.

tacking ship: To put a ship about, or change course, bringing the wind from one side of the ship around to the other side across the bow. The opposite of wearing a ship.

taking in sail: To furl a sail and secure it.

tar (British usage): Familiar term for a foremast man and an able seaman.

tar (shipboard usage): Also called "Stockholm tar," a viscous liquid of various colors, produced primarily from destructive distillation of the wood and roots of pine trees. Important to the economies of Northern Europe and Colonial America, its main use was in preserving and protecting wooden vessels and hemp rigging against rot.

tools: Hichborn's woodworking tools included an adze, caulking irons, caulking mallet, coppering hammer, maul, plane, and wrench.

top: A wooden platform, often semicircular, at the head of a lower mast. It forms a working space aloft, gives spread to the upper standing rigging, and on a warship a "fighting top" also serves as a platform for marine sharpshooters (as in the death of Lord Horatio Nelson at Trafalgar).

topping lift: A rope and/or block and tackle used to raise and support the end of a fore-and-aft sail boom.

trice: To haul up by means of a rope.

truss: An iron fitting that secures a lower yard to the mast. It is hinged to allow both vertical and horizontal movement of the yard. It incorporates a metal gooseneck that centers the yard and holds it away from the mast, so the yard can be braced at a greater angle than if it were close to the mast.

tye: That part of an upper topsail- or topgallant-yard halyard, usually made of chain, that passes over a sheave in the masthead. One end of the tye was shackled to the slings of the yard; the free end of the tye was shackled to the halyard. See also **dog.**

vang: A rope leading from the peak of the gaff of a fore-and-aft sail to the rail on each side and used for steadying the gaff.

ventilator: An opening or scoop for circulating fresh air into areas below deck.

watch: A division of time on board ship. In the merchant service, the crew is divided into two watches, port and starboard, with a mate to command each watch. The watch not on duty is known as "the watch below." Herman Melville describes these watches in chapter 79 of *White-Jacket* (1850): "The watch on duty were dozing on the carronade-slides, far above the sick-bay; and the watch below were fast asleep in their hammocks. . . ."

waterways: Long pieces of timber, running fore and aft along both sides of the ship, that connect the deck with the vessel's sides. Scuppers are cut through the waterways to drain water overboard.

wearing ship: To turn a vessel around so that the direction of the wind crosses the ship's stern. The opposite of tacking a ship.

wheel, ship's: Device used to steer the ship.

whether school keeps or not: not concerned with the consequences of one's actions.

whole go: To receive attention from the entire ship's crew.

windlass: Typically a machine with one or two horizontal spindles, erected on the foredeck of a ship, used for heavy lifting (an anchor windlass) or to heave in cables. Hichborn makes only fleeting reference to "windlass brake," so the details of *Dashing Wave's* windlass are not known. A windlass brake was essential for securing the load when lifting. See also **capstan.**

wood end: The end of a plank or board.

yard: A long spar, tapered at the ends and attached to the mast by flexible iron fittings, for supporting and spreading square sails.

"Yard, the": Refers to the Boston Navy Yard, Hichborn's former place of work.

yardarm: The tapered end of the yard.

yellow dog (doesn't know as much as a): To be stupid.

Acknowledgments

~~~~~~

Most projects of this kind require the assistance of numerous individuals and institutions. Museums and libraries that have assisted with this project include the Naval History and Heritage Command, Washington Navy Yard (Chuck Haberlein, Ed Finney, Rob Handshew); Marblehead Historical Society (Karen Mac Innis); Phillips Library, Peabody Essex Museum (Christine Michelini); Mariners' Museum Library (Claudia Jew and Tom Moore); and the San Francisco Maritime National Historic Park Library (Bill Kooiman).

I am greatly indebted to the staff members of the National Archives and Records Administration for their assistance with this project. In particular, naval and maritime archivist Mark C. Mollan has made this work possible through his strong support and encouragement. The soul of a culture lies in its history, and the United States National Archives is truly blessed to have such dedicated staff members as Mark.

I also am indebted to a number of historians for their assistance in this work. They include Coast Guard chief historian, Robert M. Browning Jr., Raymond E. Ashley, executive director of the Maritime Museum of San Diego, and my manuscript reviewers, Matthew G. McKenzie (University of Connecticut) and Douglas Jerolimov (University of Virginia). I greatly appreciate the support of *New Perspectives on Maritime History and Nautical Archaeology* series editors, James C. Bradford (Texas A&M University) and Gene Allen Smith (Texas Christian University).

I also would like to thank Meredith Morris Babb, director of the University Press of Florida, who has encouraged me in this work, as with my previous book on American shipbuilding. She is truly the guiding light for an institution that publishes some of the best work in the fields of maritime history and nautical archaeology, and her staff offered great assistance throughout the publication process. These include managing editor Gillian Hillis, senior secretary and acquisitions assistant Ebony Williams, and project editors Michele Fiyak-Burkley and Nevil Parker.

And then there is Bob Richardson. Bob served as copy editor and indexer of this book, but his investment in the project far exceeded simple copyediting. Bob and I spent many hours corresponding by e-mail and talking through content problems over the phone, so he could polish elements in the manuscript and turn my material into a more readable and edifying book. I consider myself lucky to have worked with Bob on this project.

Last, I am especially grateful to my wife Mary for her continued interest in, and assistance with, my work. Her skill and dedication in drawing illustrations and preparing photographs were essential in readying this manuscript for the publisher. I would not have succeeded in this effort without her support and encouragement.

Bibliography

~~~~~~

Contemporary Seafaring Narratives

Ames, Nathaniel. *Mariner's Sketches*. Providence, R.I.: Cory, Marshall and Hammond, 1830.

———. *Nautical Reminiscences*. Providence, R.I.: William Marshall, 1832.

Bates, Joseph. *The Autobiography of Elder Joseph Bates: Embracing A Long Life On Shipboard*. Battle Creek, Mich.: Seventh-Day Adventist Publishing Association, 1868.

Beck, Edward. *The Sea Voyages of Edward Beck in the 1820s*. Ed. Michael Hay and Joy Roberts. Edinburgh: Pentland Press, 1996.

Browne, J. Ross. *Etchings of a Whaling Cruise: With Notes of a Sojourn on the Island of Zanzibar*. Cambridge, Mass.: Harvard University Press, 1968.

Clark, George Edward. *Seven Years of a Sailor's Life*. Boston: Adams and Company, 1867.

Coffin, James Doane, Capt. *Journal of the Margaret Rait, 1840–1844*. Hantsport, Nova Scotia: Lancelot Press, 1984.

Creighton, Margaret S. *Rites and Passages: The Experience of American Whaling, 1830–1870*. Cambridge: Cambridge University Press, 1995.

Dana, Richard Henry, Jr. *Two Years before the Mast: A Personal Narrative of Life at Sea*. New York: Harper and Brothers, 1840.

Doane, Benjamin. *Following the Sea*. Halifax, Nova Scotia: Nimbus Publishing, 1987.

Froude, John W. *On the High Seas: The Diary of Capt. John W. Froude, Twillingate, 1863–1939*. St. John's, New Foundland: Jesperson Press, 1983.

Hazen, Jacob A. *Five Years before the Mast; Or, Life in the Forecastle, Aboard of a Whaler and Man-of-War*. Philadelphia: W. P. Hazard, 1854.

Little, George. *Life on the Ocean, or Twenty Years at Sea; Being the Personal Adventures of the Author*. Baltimore: Armstrong and Berry, 1843.

Leech, Samuel. *Thirty Years from Home*. Boston: Tappan and Dennet, 1843.

Lubbock, A. Basil. *Round the Horn before the Mast*. London: John Murray, 1903.

Millett, Samuel. *A Whaling Voyage in the Bark "Willis," 1849–1850*. Boston: privately printed, 1924.

Morell, Benjamin, Jr. *A Narrative of Four Voyages to the South Sea, North and South Pacific Ocean, Chinese Sea, Ethiopic and Southern Atlantic Ocean, Indian and Antarctic Ocean, from the year 1822–1831.* New York: Harper and Brothers, 1832.

Munger, James F. *Two Years in the Pacific and Arctic Oceans and China: Being a Journal of Every Day Life on board Ship.* Vernon, N.Y.: J. R. Howlett, 1852.

The Nagle Journal: A Diary of the Life of Jacob Nagle, Sailor, From the Year 1775 to 1841. Edited by John C. Dann. New York: Widenfeld and Nicolson, 1988.

Samuels, Samuel. *From the Forecastle to the Cabin: Being the Memoirs of Captain Samuel Samuels.* New York: Harper and Brothers, 1887.

Sleeper, John Sherburne. *Jack in the Forecastle; Or Incidents in the Early Life of Hawser Martingale.* New York: Crosby and Nichols Lee and Company, 1865.

Smith, Charles Edward, and Charles Edward Smith Harris. *From the Deep of the Sea: Being the Diary of the Late Charles Edward Smith.* New York: Macmillan, 1923.

Thomas, Robert. *Ship Master: The Life and Letters of Capt. Robert Thomas of Llandwrog and Liverpool, 1843–1903.* Denbigh, Wales: Gwynedd Archives Services, 1980.

Tyng, Charles. *Before the Wind: The Memoir of an American Captain, 1808–1813.* New York: Penguin, 2000.

Willard, Benjamin J. *Captain Benjamin's Book: A Record of Things Which Happened to Capt. Benjamin J. Willard, Pilot and Stevedore, During Some Sixty Years on Land and Sea.* Portland, Maine: Lakeside Press, 1895.

Primary, Secondary, and Related Sources

Bolster, W. Jeffrey. *Black Jacks: African American Seamen in the Age of Sail.* Boston: Harvard University Press, 1997.

Brighton, Ray. *Clippers of the Port of Portsmouth and the Men Who Built Them.* Portsmouth, N.H.: Portsmouth Marine Society, 1985.

Fairburn, William Armstrong. *Merchant Sail.* 6 vols. Lovell, Maine: Fairburn Marine Educational Foundation, 1945–55.

Garraty, John A., and Mark C. Carnes, eds. *American National Biography.* 24 vols. New York: Oxford University Press, 1999.

Gibson, E. Kay. *Brutality on Trial: "Hellfire" Pedersen, "Fighting" Hansen, and the Seamen's Act of 1915.* Gainesville: University Press of Florida, 2006.

Hamersly, Lewis Randolph. *The Records of Living Officers of the U.S. Navy and Marine Corps.* Philadelphia: L. R. Hamersly and Company, 1894.

Hichborn, Philip. "Chronology of the Hichborn Family, 1673–1891." Printed by the author, 1891.

————, Naval Constructor, U.S.N. *Report on European Dock-Yards.* Washington, D.C.: Government Printing Office, 1886.

Lindsey, Benjamin J. *Old Marblehead Sea Captains and the Ships in Which They Sailed.* Marblehead, Mass.: Marblehead Historical Society, 1915.

Malone, Dumas, ed. *Dictionary of American Biography.* Vol. 5, *Hibben–Larkin.* New York: Charles Scribner's Sons, 1932, 1933.

Morison, Samuel Eliot. *The Maritime History of Massachusetts, 1783–1860.* Boston: Houghton Mifflin, 1921.

"Philip Hichborn, Chief Naval Constructor, U.S.N." *Blue and Gray: The Patriotic American Magazine* 2 (July–December 1893).

Records of the Bureau of Ships. National Archives and Records Administration, Washington, D.C.

Rediker, Marcus. *Between the Devil and the Deep Blue Sea: Merchant Seamen, Pirates and the Anglo-American Maritime World, 1700–1750.* Cambridge: Cambridge University Press, 1987.

Sager, Eric W. *Seafaring Labour: The Merchant Marine of Atlantic Canada, 1820–1914.* Montreal: McGill-Queens University Press, 1996.

Shaw, David W. *Flying Cloud: The True Story of America's Most Famous Clipper Ship and the Woman Who Guided Her.* New York: HarperCollins, 2007.

Skerrett, Robert Gregg. "Philip Hichborn, Chief Constructor." *Who's Who in America.* 6th ed. (called also vol. 6). Chicago: A. N. Marquis and Company, 1910–11.

————. "Philip Hichborn, Chief Constructor, United States Navy." *Cassier's Magazine* 8, no. 1 (May–October 1895): 140–42.

Thiesen, William H. *Industrializing American Shipbuilding: The Transformation of Ship Design and Construction, 1820–1920.* Gainesville: University Press of Florida, 2006.

Vickers, Daniel. *Young Men and the Sea: Yankee Seafarers in the Age of Sail.* New Haven: Yale University Press, 2007.

Villiers, Alan. *The Way of a Ship.* New York: Charles Scribner's Sons, 1953.

Index

~~~~~~

Page numbers for glossary entries are in **boldface** and for illustrations are followed by *i*.

Philip Hichborn began his career as the ship's carpenter on *Dashing Wave* and rose through the ranks to become an admiral and the chief constructor of the U.S. Navy.

William H. Thiesen serves as historian for the U.S. Coast Guard's Atlantic Area Command. Prior to this post he served as curator of the Wisconsin Maritime Museum. He is the author of *Industrializing American Shipbuilding*.

New Perspectives on Maritime History and Nautical Archaeology

Edited by James C. Bradford and Gene Allen Smith

Maritime Heritage of the Cayman Islands, by Roger C. Smith (1999; first paperback edition, 2000)

The Three German Navies: Dissolution, Transition, and New Beginnings, 1945–1960, by Douglas C. Peifer (2002)

The Rescue of the Gale Runner: *Death, Heroism, and the U.S. Coast Guard*, by Dennis L. Noble (2002); first paperback edition, 2008

Brown Water Warfare: The U.S. Navy in Riverine Warfare and the Emergence of a Tactical Doctrine, 1775–1970, by R. Blake Dunnavent (2003)

Sea Power in the Medieval Mediterranean: The Catalan-Aragonese Fleet in the War of the Sicilian Vespers, by Lawrence V. Mott (2003)

An Admiral for America: Sir Peter Warren, Vice-Admiral of the Red, 1703–1752, by Julian Gwyn (2004)

Maritime History as World History, edited by Daniel Finamore (2004)

Counterpoint to Trafalgar: The Anglo-Russian Invasion of Naples, 1805–1806, by William Henry Flayhart III (first paperback edition, 2004)

Life and Death on the Greenland Patrol, 1942, by Thaddeus D. Novak, edited by P. J. Capelotti (2005)

X Marks the Spot: The Archaeology of Piracy, edited by Russell K. Skowronek and Charles R. Ewen (2006, first paperback edition 2007)

Industrializing American Shipbuilding: The Transformation of Ship Design and Construction, 1820–1920, by William H. Thiesen (2006)

Admiral Lord Keith and the Naval War against Napoleon, by Kevin D. McCranie (2006)

Commodore John Rodgers: Paragon of the Early American Navy, by John H. Schroeder (2006)

Borderland Smuggling: Patriots, Loyalists, and Illicit Trade in the Northeast, 1783–1820, by Joshua M. Smith (2006)

Brutality on Trial: "Hellfire" Pedersen, "Fighting" Hansen, and the Seamen's Act of 1915, by E. Kay Gibson (2006)

Uriah Levy: Reformer of the Antebellum Navy, by Ira Dye (2006)

Crisis at Sea: The United States Navy in European Waters in World War I, by William N. Still Jr. (2006)

Chinese Junks on the Pacific: Views from a Different Deck, by Hans K. Van Tilburg (2007)

Eight Thousand Years of Maltese Maritime History: Trade, Piracy, and Naval Warfare in the Central Mediterranean, by Ayşe Devrim Atauz (2007)

Merchant Mariners at War: An Oral History of World War II, by George J. Billy and Christine M. Billy (2008)

The Steamboat Montana *and the Opening of the West: History, Excavation, and Architecture,* by Annalies Corbin and Bradley A. Rodgers (2008)

Attack Transport: USS Charles Carroll *in World War II,* by Kenneth H. Goldman (2008)

Diplomats in Blue: U.S. Naval Officers in China, 1922–1933, by William Reynolds Braisted (2009)

Sir Samuel Hood and the Battle of the Chesapeake, by Colin Pengelly (2009)

Voyages, The Age of Sail: Documents in Maritime History, Volume I, 1492–1865; Volume II: The Age of Engines, 1865–Present, edited by Joshua M. Smith and the National Maritime Historical Society (2009)

Voyages, The Age of Engines: Documents in Maritime History, Volume II, 1865–Present, edited by Joshua M. Smith and the National Maritime Historical Society (2009)

H.M.S. Fowey *Lost and Found,* by Russell K. Skowronek and George R. Fischer (2009)

American Coastal Rescue Craft: A Design History of Coastal Rescue Craft Used by the United States Life-Saving Service and the United States Coast Guard, by William D. Wilkinson and Commander Timothy R. Dring, USNR (Retired) (2009)

The Spanish Convoy of 1750: Heaven's Hammer and International Diplomacy, by James A. Lewis (2009)

The Development of Mobile Logistic Support in Anglo-American Naval Policy, 1900–1953, by Peter V. Nash (2009)

Captain "Hell Roaring" Mike Healy: From American Slave to Arctic Hero, by Dennis L. Noble and Truman R. Strobridge (2009)

Sovereignty at Sea: U.S. Merchant Ships and American Entry into World War I, by Rodney Carlisle (2009)

Commodore Abraham Whipple of the Continental Navy: Privateer, Patriot, Pioneer, by Sheldon S. Cohen (2010)

Lucky 73: USS Pampanito's *Unlikely Rescue of Allied POWs in WWII,* by Aldona Sendzikas (2010)

Cruise of the Dashing Wave: *Rounding Cape Horn in 1860,* by Philip Hichborn, edited by William H. Thiesen (2010)